You GROW Girl!

Hi! I'm Gina (on the right) and I'm Kim (guess where)—proud creators of the **YGG!** workbook and program. We remember very well what it's like to be a girl, and we both have kids of our own. **YGG!** lets us share what we've learned, to help you better handle the challenging phase of life you're in.

We promise this workbook will help you if you do your part. While writing it, we often thought: "Wow, I wish I had something like this when I was this age." We loved writing it together and, frankly, we think it's really cool!

We met just a few years ago, doing what we love best—being moms. In a short time we found that we share so much in common through our families, we're already friends for life. Getting to know each other, we also discovered that we have a lot in common professionally. We both work to help kids be the best person they can be and feel GREAT in the process. Kim is a counselor in a local school district and Gina counsels kids privately.

We love being moms, being counselors, and working with kids. We love playing sports and being active. We love this workbook and encourage you to share it with others. Show your mom or other adult allies the pages that you complete. Share some of the pages with a friend. Most of all, try to love who you are and enjoy the journey of defining yourself for us all to see.

Now get ready for some fun!
Gina and Kim

You GROW Girl!™

A Self-empowering Workbook
for Tweens and Teens

Gina Scarano-Osika
Kim Dever-Johnson

LARSON PUBLICATIONS

Images reproduced by permission:
p. 10 top right, p. 57, p. 79 Lauren Cottrell; p. 14 West Hill Graphics; p. 24 photo Bill Staffeld, choreographed by Lavinia Reid; p. 82 counter ads courtesy of "Media Literacy and Popular Culture" class, Ithaca College, Cynthia Scheibe, professor.

Printed in Canada
Library of Congress Control Number: 2008931441

Publisher's Cataloging-In-Publication Data
(Prepared by The Donohue Group, Inc.)

Scarano-Osika, Gina.
   You grow girl! : a self-empowering workbook for tweens and teens / Gina Scarano-Osika,
Kim Dever-Johnson ; [foreword by Joan Jacobs Brumberg].

   p. : ill. ; cm.

Includes bibliographical references and index.
ISBN-13: 978-0-943914-73-2
ISBN-10: 0-943914-73-6

1. Teenage girls--Life skills guides. 2. Teenage girls--Health and hygiene. 3. Girls--Life skills guides. 4. Girls--Health and hygiene. 5. Self-esteem in adolescence. I. Dever-Johnson, Kim.
II. Brumberg, Joan Jacobs III. Title.

HQ798 .S337 2008
305.235/2   2008931441

Published by Larson Publications
4936 NYS Route 414
Burdett, NY 14818 USA
www.larsonpublications.com

17 16 15 14 13 12 11 10 09 08
10 9 8 7 6 5 4 3 2 1

FSC

Recycled
Supporting responsible
use of forest resources

Cert. No. SW-COC-00952
www.fsc.org
© 1996 Forest Stewardship
Council

Contents

This book is dedicated to me,

_____

So I can always remember that

I Am Beautiful!

HAPPINESS stems from taking care of my mind and my body.

CONFIDENCE grows as I get better at knowing when I have
(and have not) done my best at something.

CONTENTMENT is a fruit of accepting that my mind and body have limits.

HAPPINESS, CONFIDENCE, AND CONTENTMENT = BEAUTY

A Promise to Myself

(If you think you can't make this promise, take another look after you've read this book!)

I Promise . . .

To always remember that I am special, important, and deserve to be loved.

To love, respect, and care for myself as well as others.

To remember that the healthy choices I make today impact the habits I create all my life.

To remind myself every day that the healthy choices I make today will eventually become habits that affect how well and long I live.

To fully embrace my positive qualities and understand that everyone has weaknesses and struggles.

To try to remember that "fat" is a substance on the body and is not an appropriate way to describe myself or another person. The word "fat" is best used as a noun rather than an adjective.

To make myself a priority in my life.

To commit myself to making the connection between healthy eating attitudes and my physical health.

That each day I will try to make healthy choices that make me feel strong and good about myself.

To take the time to do what's right for my body, mind, and spirit so I can be a better friend, sister, daughter, and student.

To ask a trusted adult for help if I need some to improve how I manage my emotional and physical health.

Why this book?

Being a teenage girl can feel like a roller-coaster: one day everything sucks, the next day—maybe even the next hour—everything seems awesome and totally cool. One day, you adore a certain girlfriend, a boy, a teacher; a week later the very same person may feel like the enemy. To understand these "ups and downs" you need to know one important fact: puberty is tougher for girls than it is for boys, so girls deserve some special support.

When boys get taller and larger, they usually feel proud and impressed with themselves. Girls, on the other hand, are likely to worry about their changing bodies. As a result, they actually become more vulnerable than boys to eating disorders, substance (drug) abuse, depression, anxiety, and dropping out of school. (Girls can also get pregnant and boys can not!)

Many American girls report that they do not like their bodies, and that sets them up to be quietly unhappy and feel badly about themselves. "Bad body fever"—named by someone who has talked with thousands of American girls—is not much fun. In fact, it can be crippling. It's a lot better to be a teenage girl who likes herself and has interesting things to do than to walk around worrying about your hair, your skin, or a particular body part.

This book will help you deal with a lot of the negative stuff that is part of growing up in a world that makes how you look seem more important than what kind of person you are. The workbook has specially designed "exercises" that get you to think in a healthy, constructive way about what's bothering you. You'll also learn how to manage some of the negative, confusing feelings that get stirred up in normal teenage life, among friends at school, or even in your family.

This is not like doing homework. The examples and exercises here are not boring. And, most importantly, they will help you feel more secure and confident about what you think and feel as you move through the challenge of being an adolescent girl. Grow girls, and have fun, as you learn to focus on what your mind and body can do, rather than what you look like.

JOAN JACOBS BRUMBERG
ITHACA, NY 2008

CHAPTER 1

Self-Esteem and Body Confidence

SAMANTHA'S STORY

The waiting room was crowded with infants and preschoolers. I felt like a giant compared to these kids. "Samantha?" Finally, it was my turn to see Dr. Jackie. I couldn't wait to tell her that a few weeks ago I finally started my . . . menstrual cycle. Since my mom started hers when she was eleven, I knew I'd get mine before everyone else.

"OK, sweetheart, step on the scale," said the nurse.

My excitement turned to anguish as I watched the numbers rise . . . past 85 . . . past 90 . . . 101? "Well, that can't be right," I said. "Really, what's wrong with the scale? Let's try that one over there."

"Sam, the scale is just fine. What's wrong?"

Tears welled up in my eyes. "Last year at my physical I weighed 84. Oh my God, I had no idea! How can that be?"

"Dr. Jackie will be right in. By the way, Sam, you look grown up. Is something different?" I heard her comment, but my head was swimming with anxiety. I could only think of that dreaded NUMBER "1-0-1." I'm in the 3-digit numbers for God's sake! I screamed in my head.

After what felt like hours, Dr. Jackie knocked on the door. "Samantha! So nice to see you. Look at you! You are growing up into a beautiful young woman." I burst into tears. After I explained to her my newfound fear of the scale, she had a lot to say.

"Samantha, first of all, your body is getting ready to start your . . ."

"I already did," I interrupted. "Yes, a few weeks ago."

"Well that explains your growth over the past year. You see, Samantha, for you to menstruate, your body has to have a certain amount of body fat because body fat triggers your cycle to start. So this is a great thing!"

"I was fine until I saw that number—YUK!"

> *"I know," Dr. Jackie said. "As you get older you'll realize that scales are decep-tive and you may have to stay away from them. Especially someone like yourself, who is tall and loves to exercise. Compared to fat cells, muscle weighs three times as much! Maybe you should focus less on the numbers and more on the fact that you're healthy and you treat your body well. You look absolutely stunning."*
>
> *"Thank you," I said with a smile. And I excitedly told her all about my news.*

What Is Self-Esteem?

Self-esteem is your own measure of how pleased and at ease you are with who you are, both inside and out, regardless of what is going on around you. High self-esteem helps you feel confident and at peace, even in the most negative situations. When things in your life feel stressful and don't seem to be going your way, your mood may lower; but if you feel good about yourself, your self-esteem (for the most part) is likely to remain the same. You may think to yourself something like this: "I've had a bad day today and feel awful right now, but I still know I am a good person and I like who I am." There are many different things in your life that can help or hurt your self-esteem, so it is very important to pay attention to it.

factoid

Did you know that . . .

Low self-esteem is common among young people who use alcohol and drugs.

Role models can help you raise your self-esteem by modeling positive behaviors and attitudes. A positive role model is a person you admire. Some role models are members of your family, while others are not. Taking notice of the specific attitudes and behaviors that you most admire in that person can help you develop those traits in yourself.

In the first column on the next page, list the names of people you admire. In the second column list something you admire in them that doesn't have to do with how they look or dress.

I'd like to be like . . .

Madeleine Albright

The first female Secretary of State. In her distinguished diplomatic career she also served as the second female U.S. Representative to the United Nations, following Jeane Kirkpatrick.

Name of role model

What you admire
(not about looks)

_____   _____

_____   _____

_____   _____

_____   _____

How can you develop these admirable qualities for yourself?

_____

_____

_____

_____

_____

_____

_____

_____

Factors That Raise and Lower My Self-Esteem

When you answer these questions, think of the people, places, and things in your life that make you feel best (and worst) about yourself.

People, places, and things that **raise** my self-esteem are—

_____

_____

_____

_____

_____

_____

_____

People, places, and things that **lower** my self-esteem are—

_____
_____
_____
_____
_____
_____
_____
_____
_____

It's Good to Be Me!

As a budding young woman, you may be trying to be like others in many ways. No one likes to feel "different." Even though you may be concerned about your clothes or the style of your hair, it is important for you to know that your true beauty lies underneath your physical body. It's made up of the things that make you . . . you! That's why it's important to learn how to recognize and fully embrace your own unique qualities.

Did You Know That . . .

I'm _____ years old.

The color of my eyes is _____.

I am _____ inches tall.

The color of my hair is _____.

I have braces: ○ yes or ○ no

The thing I like the most about me is

_____
_____

My loved ones tell me I'm good at

_____
_____
_____

I like

_____   _____

_____   _____

_____   _____

_____   _____

The instrument I play is

_____

My favorite food is

_____

My favorite subject is

_____

My favorite sport or hobby is

_____

I have brothers/sisters (list)

_____   _____

_____   _____

_____   _____

_____   _____

I love these animals

_____   _____

_____   _____

_____   _____

_____   _____

List all of your good qualities

_____   _____

_____   _____

_____   _____

_____   _____

_____   _____

What is Body Confidence?

Body confidence is feeling good about how you look. Since Body Confidence refers to how you feel about your physical appearance, it does affect how you feel about yourself and can raise or lower your self-esteem.

Body Confidence can easily be damaged by focusing on how many pounds you weigh. Weight gain is very common in pre-adolescent and adolescent girls. Your body actually needs a certain amount of body fat in order to fully enter puberty. Remember also that muscle weighs much, much more than fat! So . . . only worry about your weight if your doctor is worried about your weight. Other than that . . . YOU GROW GIRL!!

Body confidence can also be damaged by images of people we see in magazines and on TV. For some professional models, maintaining their figure is their full-time job, requiring endless hours at the gym. They literally get paid millions of dollars to do it! With the additional help of professional artists and airbrushing, wrinkles, blemishes, and belly lines can easily disappear. (FYI: Sadly, some super-thin women don't carry enough body fat to fuel their reproductive system, which can result in serious medical problems.)

Body confidence can be damaged by comparing yourself to other girls. So many times, young women compare the size of their body to others, which only makes them feel awful about themselves. Girls at your age grow at very different rates. Some are taller than others and some are closer to puberty than others. Being tall and entering puberty can cause your body to grow in all kinds of different places! Comparing yourself to others is very unhealthy, both physically and emotionally. Just let YOU be YOU!!!

I'd like to be like . . .

Jackie Joyner-Kersee

Ranked among the all-time greatest heptatletes, she won 5 medals competing in the Summer Olympic Games from 1984 to 2000—three gold, one silver, and one bronze. She was the first woman to score 7,000 points in a heptathlon event at the 1986 Goodwill Games.

Now You See It . . . Now You Don't: The magic of airbrushing

Images of women on TV or in magazines can lower your **Body Confidence.** When you believe that these images are the only signs of "beauty," you define (in your mind) a beautiful person only as one who is physically beautiful. We think a beautiful person is nurturing, confident, and content. To think of beauty in only physical terms lessens the value of having a kind and warm personality.

Thinking of beauty in only physical terms is also dangerous and unhealthy, because the images we see on TV and in magazines are often not even accurate. Many pictures are "airbrushed" (modified to look much better) before they are printed. For a powerful example of this type of visual trickery, check out the "YouTube – Dove Evolution Commercial (higher quality)" video at *http://www.youtube.com/watch?v=hibyAJOSW8U&NR=1.*

For another example, compare the next two photos. Like magic, now you see IT . . . now you don't!

Between these two prints, someone has done a lot of work making the real person (on the right) look like the one on the left—who doesn't really exist! Do you want to compare the real YOU to someone who doesn't even exist?

We will talk about this kind of thing more in chapter seven.

Factors That Raise and Lower My Body Confidence

List people here to whom you physically compare yourself, in such a way that you lower your self-esteem. Explain in detail how you do this and what happens.

Person   How I do it and what happens

_____   _____

_____   _____

_____   _____

_____   _____

_____   _____

Describe the people, places, and things that raise your Body Confidence.

_____

_____

_____

_____

_____

_____

_____

_____

Describe other people, and also places and things, that lower your Body Confidence.

_____

_____

_____

_____

_____

_____

_____

Things I Want to Remember

CHAPTER 2

Food as Fuel

IZZY'S STORY

The bell rang—it was 2:30. Health class was over and it was time to go home. I tried to shake myself out of the deep thought I was in, but I couldn't. That day, my health teacher, Mrs. Nulty, had taught us about how deadly obesity is. My grandma and two aunts are very overweight, so it must run in my family. That obesity gene . . . I better be careful," I thought to myself in a determined tone.

By the time I got home I had a plan: "I'm going to be healthier so I don't become obese." The good news is that it's cross-country season so the five-mile runs after school are perfect. I followed my plan for a few weeks and then one night, at dinner, my parents told me they were concerned.

"Izzy," my mom said, "you seem nervous at dinner and when I make your favorite, macaroni and cheese, you eat a teeny tiny amount. You just don't seem like yourself. Is something wrong?"

I told my parents about what I learned in Mrs. Nulty's class and that I'm worried about becoming obese. My dad shook his head as if he knew what I was going to say. "So," he asked, "you're just trying to be more healthy, right?"

"Right," I said.

"Obesity is very scary and, yes," he said, "it runs in our family; but right now you have nothing to worry about. Your weight is fine and you exercise and eat well. However, from what I'm seeing lately, worrying about becoming obese could cause you to eat too little. Given your activity level and the fact that you're growing, eating too little can lead to very serious health risks."

My mother chimed in. "For someone your age, eating too little is just as dangerous, if not more dangerous, as being obese."

"What!" I said with my eyes as wide as saucers. "You're kidding me, right?"

"We are certainly not kidding. And what you are doing now, although for a good reason, is very dangerous. We need you to stop and go back to the way you used to eat."

"Okay, I understand . . . I just didn't know. I was so confused . . . Pass the mac 'n cheese, please!"

Metabolism and Using Food as Fuel

A nutritious diet is one in which you choose foods that provide you with all the vitamins and minerals and other good stuff your body needs to work right. Knowing which foods are the best sources of these vitamins and minerals is essential to making healthy food choices.

In addition to the food's nutritional value, how much of it you eat is also essential to your health. The best way to determine how much you should eat is to understand your body and its "metabolic rate." Metabolism is a word for a lot of processes that go on in your body and need energy. The amount of energy they need for you to remain healthy and active is measured in calories. Your "metabolic rate" is a measure of how fast or slowly your body consumes energy—how fast or how slowly you "burn calories."

The total amount of energy that a body requires in one day varies from person to person and depends upon a number of factors—such as whether you're a girl or boy, your age, and how muscular you are. Younger people require more energy than older people because younger people need extra energy to grow and successfully enter puberty. Muscular people require more energy because muscles require more energy to survive than fat cells do. That's why boys may need more food than girls. Since some people are more active than others, metabolism is different from person to person. Active people require a lot of fuel!

factoid

Did you know that . . .

The amount of energy that your body uses while you're **dreaming** is equal to the amount of energy that it uses while you're **watching TV.** Your brain requires energy to work properly, so your body burns calories both day and night . . . 24 hours a day, 7 days a week.

Understanding Serving Sizes

A "serving size" is a unit of food measured in cups or ounces. It's a specific amount of a specific food. For example, one ounce of cheese is a single "serving."

A serving size provides a specific amount of energy, as measured in calories. So, serving sizes help us determine how much energy we give our body when we eat a certain amount of a certain type of food.

The amount of food that we actually eat is called a "portion." It could be two servings of something, or it could be three or four. Knowing how many servings are in our portion, we can estimate the number of calories that we have actually eaten.

The elderly and some adults need to count serving sizes and calories in order to be sure they are not under- or over-fueling their body. Adults and the elderly use serving sizes to help determine the number of calories that they fuel their body with each day. How many "serving sizes," for example, are in the meal that they just ate, or are about to eat? By keeping track of serving sizes and calories, they can be sure to eat an appropriate "portion" of food in each meal to provide their body with just the right amount of fuel, so they can remain healthy and live long.

People typically don't eat just one serving. The amount we eat, or plan to eat is called a "portion." The "portion" of a food that we eat can be more or less than a serving size.

Unlike adults, children should NOT count calories—unless there is a concern that you are under- or over-fueling your body. If you are worried about how much fuel you are giving your body, ask your parents, the school nurse, or your pediatrician for help.

Understanding Hunger and Fullness Cues

Rather than counting calories at every meal, a healthier option is to listen to your hunger and fullness cues. Deciding when to start (and stop) eating by listening to internal hunger and fullness cues can benefit your overall health. At fast-food restaurants, where the food is tasty and the portions are HUGE, overeating is easy to do. Focusing on your internal eating cues can help. Remember, no single food causes unnecessary weight gain—but eating too much will.

The number line on the next page can help you get familiar with your hunger and fullness cues and what they feel like. Understanding it and using it can help you better notice these very important signals.

Use it to rate your level of hunger and fullness throughout the day. This will teach you how to recognize your hunger and fullness cues!

The Hunger and Fullness Scale

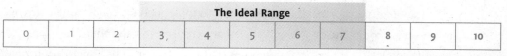

			The Ideal Range							
0	1	2	3,	4	5	6	7	8	9	10

Extreme hunger   Comfortable   **Extreme fullness**
Well **below** calorie needs   Well **above** calorie needs

Numbers on the rating scale correspond to the following feelings:

0 = extreme hunger, stabbing hunger pains, nausea, emptiness, fatigue.
Too few calories are consumed within a 24-hour period.

5 = comfortable and satisfied

10 = extreme fullness, nauseated, bloated, uncomfortably full.
Too many calories are consumed within a 24-hour period.

Listen to your fullness and hunger cues so you can start and stop eating depending upon how you feel.

Any time you ignore your hunger pains (0, 1, 2), you run the risk of not giving your body the fuel it needs. This may make you feel dizzy, empty, starved, or nauseated at certain points in your day.

Likewise, if you feel overfull much of the day (8, 9, 10) you may be giving your body too much fuel over the course of a day. This, too, is unhealthy and can make you feel "stuffed," nauseated, and uncomfortably full.

Staying within the Ideal Range is optimal for your health. That is, start eating when you feel you are at a 3 and stop before you get to a 7. Healthy eating begins when you feel empty, start thinking about food, or have hunger pains. Eating when you are hungry is essential to giving your body enough fuel. Since your stomach only holds a little bit of food at one time, eating slowly is important so you can pay attention to your internal fullness cues. You may realize that there comes a point when you feel full, but continue eating anyway because the food tastes so good. Be careful!

So, looking at the Hunger and Fullness Scale, it is healthiest if you stop eating when you are at a 5, because 20 minutes later you may be at a 7 or 8.

factoid

Did you know that . . .

You will continue to feel more and more full for an entire 20 minutes after the time you have STOPPED eating!!!

Dancers and performers

Everything we've said so far applies to everyone, but it especially applies to dancers who may be told they need to lose weight to look good on stage. Your body needs to be very strong, and to get and stay that way it needs abundant nutrients from healthy foods. It happens way too often that girls trying to be super-thin for ballet (or other forms of dance) don't eat enough of the right things for their bodies to be able to do (or to keep doing) what they need to do. It's one of the reasons dancers can be injury prone.

If any adult tells you that you need to lose weight for a part in a performance, and you feel that is unhealthy or it makes you feel weak, consult with a professional nutritionist. Remember: If you eat healthfully, your weight will settle where it needs to be for your age and activity level.

Healthy Eating Attitudes

What are healthy eating attitudes? Healthy eating includes:

1. Eating when hungry and stopping when full
2. Feeling comfortable eating a wide variety of foods
3. Being able to enjoy rich foods without guilt or anxiety
4. Eating according to internal cues, not external circumstances (such as time of day or the company you keep)
5. Eating to celebrate or be social
6. Not allowing "shoulds" to determine what and how much you eat
7. Eating solely for pleasure
8. Eating because you are happy, sad, bored, or just because it feels good
9. Looking forward to eating out without fear or guilt
10. Eating more now because it tastes wonderfully fresh
11. Trusting your body to make up for mistakes in eating
12. Not allowing food or weight issues to become your only focus in life
13. Leaving uneaten food on your plate
14. Overeating on special occasions with guilt-free minimal weight gain
15. On occasion, overeating to cope with stress with minimal weight gain
16. A reduction or increase in appetite when under stress
17. Eating just because the food is there and it smells good
18. Improving health habits if your weight goes above a BMI* of 29
19. Gaining weight and improving health habits if your BMI* falls below 20
20. Maximizing healthy behaviors if you have a BMI* of 20–29

*Body Mass Index

The body mass index (BMI) relates a person's height and weight in a way that helps estimate how much body fat they have, but it's more useful for adults than for kids. It's also not accurate for very muscular people. It can help predict possible health risks, and is worth mentioning for that reason.

Underweight BMI less than 18.5	Overweight BMI 25 – 30
Normal BMI 18.5 – 25	Obese BMI more than 30

Things I Want to Remember

Way to Go!

JENNA'S STORY

The national anthem was playing full out at the Olympic games. I had won the gold medal in the all-around competition in women's gymnastics. The crowd roared . . . banners were waving, wishing me well, "We love you Jenna!" chanted the crowd . . .

"BEEP! BEEP! BEEP! BEEP! BEEP!" The clock read 5:30 a.m. It was time to start another day.

By 6:30 I was dressed perfectly and my hair was sleek (it better have been—I spent 30 minutes with a flat iron!). I grabbed a granola bar and a few other things for lunch. Oh yeah, I thought, my lunch has to be quick today because I need to finish my chemistry homework. I put the granola bar back.

School starts at 7:10. No study halls. Choir. Band practice. Five classes and AP English. I'd love to catch Jessica and make plans for the weekend, but I have to get to lunch and do my chemistry. In a blink of an eye, the day is over.

It's 2:30 and I need to get extra help in English—I only got an 89 on my last composition so I need to ask my teacher how to make it better. I'll be a bit late for gymnastics practice, but maybe I'll stay late to make it up. I do need extra practice on my floor routine if I'm going to make it to Sectionals.

5:00 p.m. and I'm starving. We drive through Burger King and I could easily eat a Whopper and fries. I hardly ate all day. I opt for the chicken salad . . . remember Sectionals.

6:00 p.m. and I'm ready to start my homework. The good news is that I only have three hours of homework tonight . . . one hour practicing my flute lesson . . . maybe an hour IM'ing to relax. I can skip lunch again tomorrow to do my chemistry, that seems to work well . . . Shoot! Mrs. Pratt (my guidance counselor) wants me to meet with her tomorrow during lunch. I better get to work. More of the same until the next day at lunch.

Knock . . . Knock . . . Knock . . . "Come in Jenna," calls Mrs. Pratt from her desk. She always looks so busy. "Have a seat."

"You're probably wondering why I wanted to meet with you today. Well, I have to say that I'm worried."

"It's my grades," I blurt out. "I know my last English grade was . . ."

"Jenna," she interrupts, "this has nothing to do with your grades. This has to do with you." I must look confused because she sits back in her chair and takes a deep breath. "I think you are trying to carry too much this semester."

"What do you mean?" I ask.

"Well, I see the schedule you keep, and I just think it's unhealthy. It doesn't leave you enough time to relax and just be a kid."

"But what class will I drop? . . . How will I . . . What do I tell my parents?" These thoughts swim in my head. What I say next surprises me.

"Is that why I'm so tired all the time? I never feel good about myself."

"Yes, Jenna. You're the type of student who pushes herself too much. You are so preoccupied with what you didn't do well enough, you never focus on all that you do well. Please tell your parents about our discussion and come back tomorrow so we can re-work your schedule."

"Thank you, Mrs. Pratt. I've been so busy I never realized how awful I always feel."

I left her office, had a nice big lunch, and asked for an extension on my chemistry homework. As I walked outside to my next class, I heard the birds chirping and the smell of spring was in the air. I looked around and saw other kids laughing and having fun. "I want to do that."

And I did.

The Power of Positive Thinking on Self-Esteem

Negative thoughts can lower self-esteem, which is stressful to both your mind and body. In fact, negative thinking and emotional stress are known to cause depression and medical illnesses such as obesity and diabetes. How you think about a situation affects your self-esteem and how you feel about yourself. When you think of phrases like "I never," "I can't," or "I should," there is a good chance that you will end up feeling bad about yourself.

On the next page, read about each situation and make note of how positive and negative thoughts can make you feel. Write the feeling in the line after the description. If you need help identifying feelings, choose from the following list.

Happy	Confident	Joyful	Encouraged	Peaceful	Content
Nurtured	Respected	Cherished	Hopeful	Guilty	Relieved
Sad	Depressed	Helpless	Angry	Disappointed	Frustrated
Betrayed	Tired	Paranoid	Lonely	Rejected	Worried/Anxious

Situation A

In gym class we were climbing rope but I only made it up one-fourth of the way.

Negative Thoughts

    I'm the weakest kid in the class.

    I hate myself.

    What's the use of trying anymore?

Feelings

_____

_____

_____

Positive Thought

    Although I need to work on my arm strength,

    I have to remember that my strongest sport is

_____.

Feelings

_____

Situation B

My grades have slipped, especially in math.

Negative Thoughts

    I must be stupid.

    What's the use of trying anymore?

    I may as well stop trying, this is too much work.

Feelings

_____

_____

_____

Positive Thoughts

    Math is a subject that doesn't come easily to me.

    Everyone has subjects with which they struggle.

    I need to accept my weaknesses as a challenge.

Feelings

_____

_____

_____

Situation C

I really get nervous and panicky when I'm around certain (groups of) people.

Negative Thoughts

They must be saying bad things about me.

No one likes me.

I don't fit in with anyone.

Feelings

_____

_____

_____

Positive Thoughts

Maybe I should talk to an adult about these kids so I can be sure that I have things in common with them. That will help me relax.

As long as I pay attention to my interests, I will find my "place" within a social group.

Feelings

_____

_____

Situation D

Many girls are much smaller than me.

Negative Thoughts

I'm "fat."

No one likes me.

They must think I am too big.

Feelings

_____

_____

_____

Positive Thought

At my age kids grow at different rates. My health is most important so I need to accept the way my body is growing and focus only on my health.

Feelings

_____

The Power of Positive Thinking on Body Confidence

Negative thoughts about your body can make you feel ashamed of how you look. When you look in the mirror, these negative thoughts and feelings can also make you see a distorted image of yourself. The result is low Body Confidence.

Negative Thoughts
+
Negative Feelings
=
Negative Perception

Read the statements that follow and try to understand how healthy and unhealthy thought patterns make you feel. Write the feeling on the line following the description. Use the following list of feelings for help.

Happy	Confident	Joyful	Encouraged	Peaceful	Content
Nurtured	Respected	Cherished	Hopeful	Guilty	Relieved
Sad	Depressed	Helpless	Angry	Disappointed	Frustrated
Betrayed	Tired	Paranoid	Lonely	Rejected	Worried/Anxious

Situation A

Girls are discussing jeans sizes and body weight. Many of them wear smaller sizes than me.

Unhealthy Thoughts

I hate my body.

Since I'm bigger I must be "fat."

I'm too big for any boy to ever like me.

Feelings

_____

_____

_____

Healthy Thoughts

They may be late "bloomers" and their growth will catch up in a year or two.

Weight gain and growth during puberty is a sign of a healthy body.

I have gained weight because I have been growing, not because I have gained fat, necessarily.

Feelings

_____

_____

_____

Situation B

Shannon recently lost a lot of weight and everyone is paying attention to her. All the boys seem to think she is pretty.

Unhealthy Thoughts	Feelings
Maybe I should lose weight like her.	_____
I'm too big for any boy to like me	_____
I wish I looked like her.	_____

Healthy Thoughts	Feelings
I know some boys who like me just as I am.	_____
For many kids, weight loss is dangerous.	_____
I'm worried about my friend, maybe I should get some help from the school nurse.	_____

Situation C

One of my friends doesn't eat much of her lunch. She just watches me eat mine.

Unhealthy Thoughts	Feelings
Maybe I shouldn't eat so much at lunch.	_____
Since I eat more I must be "fat."	_____
I feel "fat."	_____

Healthy Thoughts	Feelings
Skipping meals is unhealthy.	_____
I'm worried about my friend, maybe I should get some help from the school nurse.	_____
My friend may be afraid to eat, wishing she looked like me.	_____

Situation D

I had chocolate chip cookies in my lunch bag today and my friend told me they were "bad."

Unhealthy Thoughts

    Since I eat cookies I must be "fat."

    Maybe I shouldn't eat cookies any more."

    I feel "fat."

Feelings

_____

_____

_____

Healthy Thoughts

    I'm worried about my friend, maybe I should get some help from the school nurse, or maybe from our guidance counselor or a teacher.

Feelings

    Eating a few cookies is healthy as long as my diet is nutritious and balanced the rest of the day.

_____

    No single food causes weight gain, but eating too much will.

_____

The A-BE-C's of Stress Management and Coping

The following four problem-solving steps increase self-esteem by increasing self-awareness, controlling negative behaviors, and strengthening assertiveness skills. Problem-solving can give you a sense of being powerful which promotes both emotional and physical wellness.

    First we will look at the whole approach. Then in the next section we will do an exercise with it.

1. Awareness and Insight: What Do I Need?

Asking these six questions can be very helpful when you have a problem.

Who is the problem?

What is the problem?

Where is the problem?

Why is there a problem?

When does the problem occur?

What do you need?

2. Behavioral Control

Visualize the consequences of acting on your emotions right now. Will you hurt someone's feelings? Will you do something that you might regret later? Is there a possibility that you could get disciplined for your behavior? How will the consequence feel?

3. Emotional Expression

How Do You Feel?

0	5	10
Unemotional	**Self-Awareness**	**Overemotional**
Ignoring feelings	**Self-Control**	**Saying or doing things you regret**

5 is the most productive place to be

Emotional expression is important to self-esteem and coping. Feelings can be your "friend" if you listen to them. However, you may not always want to "do," or act the way your feelings tell you to. Acting on, or expressing your feelings when your feelings are intense and powerful can lead to unhealthy decisions. So when you are at a "10," take a time-out to calm yourself down and get your thoughts together.

On the other hand, not paying attention to your feelings can prevent you from learning about a situation and understanding it better. Feelings are very personal and private, and no one should ever tell you that your feelings are wrong. Feelings are best if shared with only your "safest" of friends—those who listen to you and respect how you feel. Feel free to pick and choose what you say or how much you say to each individual person.

4. Communicating Needs

Develop a plan.

What do you want to say?

When do you want to say it?

Focus on feelings because they can't be "wrong." How do you feel?

What does the person say/do that makes you feel bad?

What changes can you both make to help the situation get better?

My Problems and My Coping Skills

In this section, use the four-step A-BE-C model to help you cope with a problem or conflict you are currently experiencing.

1. Awareness & Insight: What Do I Need?

Describe a current problem you are having.

Who is the problem?

_____

_____

What is the problem?

_____

_____

_____

_____

Where is the problem?

_____

_____

_____

Why is there a problem?

_____

_____

When does the problem occur?

_____

_____

What do you need?

_____

_____

_____

_____

_____

_____

2. Behavioral Control

Visualize the consequences of acting on your emotions right now. Will you hurt someone's feelings? Will you do something that you might regret later? Is there a possibility that you could get disciplined for your behavior? How will the consequence feel?

_____

_____

_____

_____

_____

_____

3. Emotional Expression

Describe how you feel regarding this situation when your feelings are most intense.

· ·

0   5   10

Unemotional   **Self-Awareness**   **Overemotional**

Ignoring feelings   **Self-Control**   **Saying or doing things you regret**

5 is the most productive place to be

How Do You Feel?

_____

_____

_____

_____

_____

Not sure? Then:

    Write in your journal

    Talk with a friend or parent

    Listen to music or read

    Clarify how you feel and why

4. Communicating Needs

Develop a plan.

What do you want to say?

_____

_____

_____

_____

_____

When do you want to say it?

_____

_____

_____

Focus on feelings because they can't be "wrong." How do you feel?

_____

_____

_____

_____

What does the person say/do that makes you feel bad?

_____

_____

_____

_____

What changes can you both make to help the situation get better?

_____

_____

_____

_____

The Power of Your Own A-BE-C's

You can get to your A-BE-C's of many different problems with this approach. It can be something as simple as how to find time to do a boring homework assignment, or how to get over a little fight with a friend. Or it can be something very complicated. See pages 97–107 in Appendix D, for example, for samples of how you can use it to sort out who you want to be in stressful situations involving sexuality, alcohol, or drugs.

Things I Want to Remember

_____

_____

_____

_____

_____

_____

_____

_____

_____

CHAPTER 4

Get Moving!

AMY'S STORY

I was the first one home after school. The house was quiet . . . but it wouldn't be for long.

Dear Amy,

Please be sure to feed the kids around 4:00 and remember that Sarah has a project due tomorrow. I'll be home around 7:00.

Love, Mom

You see, I'm the oldest of six kids and my dad left us about five years ago. My mom works a lot—she has to. So I have to help out A LOT. Don't get me wrong, of course I want to help out, but I'm getting tired of it. My life feels out of balance.

I did my usual thing. I only had 45 minutes of peace and quiet. I grabbed a box of cookies and watched my favorite TV show. I don't remember much, but I did feel good . . .

"HEY AMY! Let me in!" roared my brother. I trudged to the door and my brother burst through. "Didn't you hear me?" I just grunted. Within 30 minutes, the other four kids came home from school. They were all hungry and tired, and I couldn't have cared less.

While I lay in bed that night I promised myself that something had to change. "I can't do this anymore," I thought to myself. Then the helplessness. I can't ask my mom for help, she already has enough to worry about. I can't get away from the house because I have to watch the kids. All I know is that something has to change . . . but how?

The next day I sat with my teacher and told her about my unhappiness. I was nervous but I did it anyway. She listened to me and made me feel like she could help. The next day my gym teacher, Mr. Leonard, took me aside and told me about an after-school activity club that he would like me to join. I could take the late bus home and still be home in time to watch the kids. The club sounded fun. I could meet some friends and get some exercise as well.

"Sign me up!" I said. "But what about my mom?"

"I'll talk to her," said Mr. Leonard.

The next day, my 45 minutes of cookies and TV were replaced with movement and laughter. It's been that way for a month, and I'm amazed at how much happier I am. I enjoy watching my brothers and sisters when I get home, and I have so much more energy. I'm so glad that I asked for help!

factoid

Did you know that . . .

The daily activity requirement of our ancestors was equal to a 2.5 mile walk. For centuries, people had to move in order to meet their needs for food and water. Distant streams and rivers were the main source of water. Meat had to be hunted. Produce had to be harvested. So different than what we are used to today! Nowadays, food is within steps of us, every minute of every day.

Everyone knows that exercise is good for you. You hear it all the time! However, the reality is that sometimes it can be boring, so you don't do it as much as you should. When you don't feel like exercising, you need to read this section in order to Get Moving!

The Impact of Stress on Your Body

Many people think that being a kid is easy, but all young people have stress in their life. Academic pressure, peer pressure, and family conflict are just a few of the many things that can cause you to feel stressed, anxious, or sad.

Scientists are learning more and more about the connection between your mind and your body. When you feel stressed, your body makes invisible and internal changes in order to cope. These changes are sometimes dangerous if they remain in place for a long time. For example, when your mind is stressed, your body produces its own energy and fuel in the form of blood sugar. So, without eating a single bite of food, your body feeds on itself. This sugar remains in your bloodstream and, over time, can cause medical conditions such as diabetes, high cholesterol, and obesity.

factoid

Did you know that . . .

Exercise is the best way to lower blood sugar and counteract the negative effects of stress.

Exercise is More Than Just Activity

Do you remember our discussion about metabolism in chapter 2 on Food as Fuel? Metabolism is what determines the amount of energy your body uses during the course of a day, to energize your mind and body. Your lungs, heart, brain, and muscles all require energy to function. Food provides your body with that energy, just like gas fuels a car.

If you provide your body with too much fuel, your body stores the extra energy in the form of fat. Too much fat can be dangerous and unhealthy. Some people try to eat less, to control how much fat they store on their body. This is difficult to do all the time because food tastes good and is abundant in the world we live in. By reading this section, you will learn that exercising is a better way to control how much fat your body stores.

factoid

Did you know that . . .

Rather than **lower** the amount of energy (food) that you give your body, **increase** the amount of energy that your body uses each day—it's a much healthier option.

If you get one hour of activity a day, your body will require more fuel (and make fat storage less likely) than if you get only five minutes of activity. The more activity your body gets, the heavier it will be, because muscle weighs more than fat. Muscular bodies require more energy than less muscular bodies, making fat storage less likely. So, rather than lowering the amount of energy that you give your body, use up all the fuel you give it instead. That way there isn't any fuel left over for storage.

Let's use a car as an example of how to increase the amount of energy that your body requires. If a car is driven 20 miles in one day, it will use more gasoline (energy) than if it is driven only five miles. Plus, if a car carries three grown men, it will use more fuel than if it carries three young children.

Exercise for Enjoyment

Being active can be fun! It will make you strong and help you relieve stress in a positive way. The important thing to remember is to find activities you enjoy and try to do a little of those each day. This will help you develop healthy habits that will last you a lifetime.

Some examples of activity include: Taking a walk with a friend or pet, going swimming, riding your bike, roller skating, planting flowers, dancing to music, taking a hike, running, using a hula-hoop . . . The list is endless! Remember to mix it up a little. Variety is the key so you won't get bored.

I enjoy these activities:

_____   _____
_____   _____
_____   _____
_____   _____
_____   _____
_____

I am talented at these skills, activities, or sports:

_____   _____
_____   _____
_____   _____
_____   _____
_____   _____

I would like to try these activities:

_____   _____
_____   _____
_____   _____
_____   _____
_____   _____

Kids are busy people. Sports, homework, and social time are all important to having a balanced life. Because of this, scheduling physical exercise can be difficult.

The best days of the week for me to be active are . . .

_____   _____
_____   _____
_____   _____
_____

Why?

_____
_____
_____

The best times of day for me to be active are . . .

_____   _____
_____   _____
_____

Why?

_____
_____
_____

I'd like to be like . . .

Mae Jamison, M.D.

She became the first Black woman to travel in space when she went into orbit aboard the Space Shuttle _Endeavour_ on September 12, 1992. She is a chemical engineer, scientist, physician, teacher, astronaut and has trained in dance and choreography

Ask for Help

Needing and wanting to be more active is sometimes not so easy. Nighttime schedules are hectic. Parents sometimes work late. Extreme weather conditions make it difficult to get outside to play. Here are some ideas to help you Get Moving!

1. Ask Your Friends for Help

Recess is a great time to ask your friends to play games that involve a lot of running. Playgrounds make great obstacle courses and relay races are a fine way to get your heart pumping.

At home, your friends can be a wonderful source of fun and activity. Soccer, jumping rope, basketball, touch football, and bike riding are all aerobic activities—which means that as you make your body stronger, you also make your heart stronger.

Which friends are best to help you get moving?

_____   _____
_____   _____
_____   _____

Do you have an older brother or sister who can help you get moving? Who?

_____   _____
_____   _____

2. Ask Your Parents or Step-parents for Help

Although you may want to get more activity, you may need to have an adult to be with you in order to be safe. You may need supervision on the playground or transportation to where you want to exercise.

For you to get more physical activity, which parent, step-parent, guardian, or grandparent may you need to ask for help?

_____   _____
_____   _____

Are you afraid to ask him or her? _____

If yes, what are you afraid of?

_____

_____

3. Ask Another Trusted Adult for Help

If your parents aren't able to help you increase your level of activity, you may want to speak with a trusted adult—a member of your extended family, maybe, or your (gym?) teacher, the school nurse or counselor. Although you may be nervous about asking them for help, remember that you do come into contact with many adults, especially at school, who are very willing to help—and want you to GET MOVING!

Which trusted adult might help you get moving?

_____   _____
_____   _____

When can you ask them for help? _____

Do you want a friend or sibling to help you ask this trusted adult?
If so, which friend or sibling?

_____   _____
_____   _____
_____   _____

Things I Want to Remember

_____
_____
_____
_____
_____
_____
_____
_____
_____
_____
_____

Five Lessons from a Highly Effective Teenage Drama Queen

(Who Needed to Learn How to Plug into Herself)

Isn't there an old saying "Once a drama queen, always a drama queen"? Well if there isn't, there should be. We all know them. They fill our lives with chaos and conflict, and wreak emotional havoc wherever they go. And, to be honest, who among us doesn't have her own drama queen inside herself to contend with?

I'll never forget the day I first asked a teenager, "Umm ... what exactly *is* a drama queen?" After that, the word became a part of just about every conversation I had with a teenage girl. THEY ARE EVERYWHERE ... but chances are ... they are saying that YOU are the drama queen. They play those mind games ya know. And sometimes they may even be right, right?

The goal of this chapter is to set the record straight and outline what a "Drama Queen" is and what a "Drama Queen" is not. This chapter will also help you cope and be patient with the Drama Queens in your life and inside yourself.

1. Drama Queens Say and Do Things that Create Drama

They may be popular ... boys may look at them more than at you ... but in reality, they have no clue how to be a true friend. They may be outwardly "beautiful," but they lack important internal qualities: generosity, compassion, and empathy (the ability to understand how others feel), for example. They may lie to get what they want because they don't really know how to communicate. They start rumors about you and post them on the Internet for all to see. They may do hurtful things when they are upset because they don't know any better. They may blame you for things or start rumors about you in order to get out of a tough situation. They may even pretend to be you when IM'ing your boyfriend. All you know is that you just don't feel comfortable—like yourself—when you are around them. (Or when you act like them, and who doesn't sometimes?)

Everyone has needs. The difficult part is to realize what your needs are and how to get your needs met. Have you noticed that this is easy to do with some people and almost impossible to do with others? Because of being disconnected with themselves and others, Drama Queens don't understand the needs of others. Making even the simplest arrangements with a Drama Queen can feel like a tug-of-war, because a Drama Queen doesn't understand that others can be needy, too. Some Drama Queens even hate it when others are needy.

Drama Queens excel at talking negatively about others. They love being the center of attention, especially when telling a story about someone else. They critique people, criticize clothing, and pick apart special occasions. They rain on everyone's parade.

Here are six questions that can help you determine who the Drama Queen(s) are in your life.

A. Do you know anyone who lies in order to get what they want, despite saying that they are your "friend"?

    If yes, who?   _____

    What did they lie about? _____

B. Who in your life seems to continue to do things or say things to you that hurt your feelings?

_____ _____

_____ _____

C. Does anyone in your life blame you when things go wrong? Who?

_____ _____

_____ _____

D. When you are needy, who listens the best? Name three people:

1. _____

2. _____

3. _____

E. When you are needy, who listens the worst? Name three people.

1. _____

2. _____

3. _____

F. Name three people you have heard say mean or rude things about another person.

1. _____

2. _____

3. _____

2. Drama Queens Are Smart . . . but Sometimes Unwise

As you mature into a happy and healthy young woman, you will come to understand the difference between intellect and wisdom. They may sound similar, but in fact they are very different. Intellect is the ability to think about and remember what you've read or seen or been told. Intellectual people are quick to complete their homework and may get very good grades. Although they are "smart," that doesn't necessarily mean they have wisdom.

Wisdom is the ability to solve complex real-life problems by integrating many different factors. A wise person will look at a problem from many different perspectives and make a determination only after all factors are taken into account.

This applies equally to adults and kids. Let's say a person is going on a vacation and they are driving to their destination. At the time of their planned departure, they realize that a snow storm is upon them. A smart person may leave at the predetermined time, regardless of the weather and without any alteration in their plans. (I don't think this is smart, but I do know smart people who have done it!)

A wise person, on the other hand, may take into consideration the inclement weather and make a healthier, less risky decision. A wise person may alter the driving route, leave a day later, or reserve a hotel room shortly into the trip (just in case). Smart people sometimes don't make healthy or wise decisions.

An important difference between wisdom and intellect is in the use of drugs and alcohol. Many "smart" teenagers may use drugs and alcohol, despite proven health consequences. They actually think they are immune, that nothing can hurt them. People who don't use drugs or alcohol are not only smart, they are wise as well—because they think about the future and have a broader perspective than just the moment.

Wise girls don't fad diet. Similar to the tobacco industry, the dieting industry is slow to admit the dangers of fad dieting. The fact is, however, that fad dieting among young girls is dangerous—it can result in adulthood illnesses such as depression, anorexia, and even obesity. In addition to Mother's Against Drunk Driving (MADD), I wish we could develop a following for Mother's Against Dieting (MAD). A wise teenager accepts that she may have negative thoughts and feelings about her body, but knows that these really are temporary blips on the radar of her mind.

The following five questions will help you determine which of your friends are wise and which are not.

A. Name three things that you were asked by a friend to do or say, that may have been unwise.

1. _____

2. _____

3. _____

How did you feel about this afterwards?

_____

_____

_____

B. Name the friends that asked you to do or say these things OR who initiated that idea to begin with.

1. _____

2. _____

3. _____

4. _____

5. _____

C. Name two things that you currently feel pressure to do or say that may be unwise.

1. _____
2. _____

D. Name three things you can do in order to be wiser.

1. _____
2. _____
3. _____

E. Name three things you can stop doing in order to be wiser.

1. _____
2. _____
3. _____

F. Think of three reasons why fad diets are unwise.

1. _____
2. _____
3. _____

3. Wise People "Sit and Go Blah"

My grandmother was sweet and very much to-the-point. She was the type of person who would pull aside teenage boys at the mall and chastise them for not holding the door open for the new mom who just strolled by with her newborn. She was always moving, even during meals . . . just in case someone needed something, she was ready to go.

But every day she would "go blah." She'd stop moving . . . sit in her chair . . . lean her head back . . . and close her eyes. "I'm not sleeping," she'd say—as if sleeping were a bad thing to do in the middle of the afternoon.

When I'd call her from college, she'd ask me, "Did you go blah today?" Many times I lied and said yes. I wish I knew then what I know now.

Now I realize that she wasn't going blank or numb (like some people try to do in a variety of not-so-wise ways). She was releasing her body of its stress, freeing her mind of its contents . . . letting thoughts, fears, doubts go . . . calming herself, re-centering in her deep sense of herself. It's how she recovered her clarity, recharged her batteries. It's why she could also Get up and Go whenever and however that was needed, at the drop of a hat.

It's also how she knew when to just let something go if it didn't concern her, or if there was nothing she could do about it at the time. It kept her in touch with "the big picture."

I've since learned that LOTS of people make time to center themselves in one way or another. Do you know anyone who does? Someone in your family?

_____

_____

Or a teacher or friend?

_____

_____

Maybe a celebrity you've read about or heard about?

_____

_____

HINT: Which of these people does it?*

 Madonna   Oprah   Penelope Cruz

*(*answer: all of them!)*

An informal survey of girls aged 10 to 16 suggests that—like me when I was in school—they don't "go blah" either. We asked them: "Besides at bedtime, how many minutes a day do you spend in complete silence?" They said that on average they spend about six minutes a day in complete silence.

We asked how much they like doing this sort of thing and they said they like sitting in silence "only somewhat"—rating it a 5.4 out of 10. A few of the girls made notes on the survey saying that they are made to sit in silence and don't want to at all.

On a scale of 0 to 10, how often do YOU enjoy quiet or alone time? Put a mark in the appropriate number range below.

0   5   10

Can't Stand   **Somewhat**   **All the time**

Learning how to "Sit and Go Blah" will help you cleanse your mind and feel comfortable in your own skin. With so many distractions, electronics, computers, block scheduling, and iPods, it is very difficult to be alone without some sort of entertainment. But like my grandmother said, "Going blah is as important as eating and sleeping." Why?

1. It gives your mind time to catch up on the events of the day.

2. It helps you re-think the day and make creative connections.

3. It lets you focus and concentrate on how your body really feels.

4. It can help you remember things you almost forgot.

5. It can help you be better in tune with a loved one from whom
   you have felt detached.

The following five questions will help you "sit and go blah" on a regular basis.

A. What are the feelings or events that you experience that make you feel most stressed?

1. _____

2. _____

3. _____

4. _____

5. _____

When you experience these things, you may feel better if you "sit and go blah."

B. Where is the best place for you to "sit and go blah"? Why?

_____

_____

_____

C. What time(s) of day would you be most available to "sit and go blah"?

_____   _____

_____   _____

D. What factors prevent you from relaxing more?

_____

_____

_____

_____

_____

E. What do you need in order to "sit and go blah" more frequently?

_____

_____

_____

_____

_____

I'd like to be like . . .

Maya Angelou

Author, poet laureate, playwright and civil rights activist. Angelou recited her poem, "On the Pulse of Morning" at President Bill Clinton's inauguration in 1993. She has received over thirty honorary degrees.

For extra credit

Here are a few tips than can help you majorly sit and go blah when you do find time to try it. Get into a comfortable position in a soothing place and

1. Relax your body.

Can you just observe what your body feels like? Where does it feel pain, or tightness? What happens when you just pay attention to the pain? Is it gritty? or sharp? or deep and achy, or . . .? Can you just notice the sensation, and not react to it?

List places in your body that don't feel right to you, and what kind of discomfort is there.

_____   _____

_____   _____

List places in your body that feel good, where you are comfortable.

_____   _____

_____   _____

_____   _____

_____   _____

2. Calm your mind.

If you're like most of us, your mind is probably racing with thoughts most of the time. Can you see which thoughts are racing in your mind at the moment?

_____   _____
_____   _____
_____   _____
_____   _____
_____   _____

Any chance you could just let them be, and relax?

Sometimes it helps if you just watch your breathing. Start by watching a breath come in (through your nose is better) . . . pay attention the whole time as it comes in. Just watch it, don't interfere. Then watch it go out . . . all the way . . . all by itself. Then do it a few more times. Or as many as you want. Just watching. Have you ever tried this? What happens when you do?

_____
_____
_____
_____
_____

3. Center yourself.

Much of what disturbs us or makes us unhappy comes from outside ourselves. What do you feel is coming from inside yourself? Can you even find where "inside yourself" is?

What happens when you pay attention to "inside yourself"?

_____
_____
_____
_____

4. Soak up the good energy.

When you are alert, centered, and comfortable inside yourself, do you feel a good energy around you or coming up from inside you? Soak it up! And then when you go back to whatever you have to do—spread it around!

List three times when you have felt a positive, bright energy around you or inside you.

1. _____

2. _____

3. _____

What did you do with the energy?

_____
_____
_____
_____

Did you spread it around? _____

If you did, what happened?

_____
_____
_____
_____

If you didn't, why not?

_____
_____
_____
_____

4. Wise People Are Mindful: They "let go" of Unhealthy Thoughts and Feelings

Mindfulness helps you develop an ability to be aware of external circumstances while at the same time accepting your instinctual thoughts and feelings about each circumstance. When stressed, a mindful person pays attention to all the different aspects of that situation and all the different reactions they have to the stress. Because a mindful person is aware of multiple factors, they are able to make healthier decisions and not get "carried away" with untrue thoughts or intense feelings. A wise person thinks critically about their thoughts and feelings and "lets go" of any thought, feeling, or situation that does not lead to a healthy decision.

A wise person is level-headed; they acknowledge intense feelings and negative thoughts, but they don't act on them blindly. A wise person knows that all people have unhealthy thoughts and feelings and that these unhealthy thoughts and feelings can happen automatically—without even thinking about it. Although a mindful person knows that they are capable of unhealthy thoughts and feelings, the mindful person enjoys the challenge of picking and choosing which thoughts or feelings to "let go" and ignore, and which to embrace.

Drama Queens, on the other hand, are not mindful; they let their thoughts and feelings get "carried away." A Drama Queen may start to study for a test and think, "I'm anxious about the test tomorrow" and then be crippled with fear and anxiety to the point that she can't study. A Drama Queen may think, "I'm so bored with studying, maybe I shouldn't study anymore." Or, she may "invent" or fabricate situations that keep her from studying.

In contrast, a mindful person may feel anxious about the test but let go of these feelings so that they can study. A mindful person may feel bored while studying, but know that if she pays attention to that feeling she won't learn as well during the study session. A mindful person can let these uncomfortable feelings "go" and replace them with a healthy and constructive thought. Whereas an unwise person may not study because of the boredom, a wise person will realize that listening to this feeling will result in an unhealthy behavior.

A wise person will feel full after a large meal and never assume that she's fat. A wise person can feel full without assuming that the fullness means she's too large. She lets that "fat" feeling go and reminds herself that she's just full, and fullness is a temporary experience. A wise person knows that even if there's food left on her plate, if she feels full, she should probably stop eating. She avoids further discomfort by paying attention to feeling full and "letting go" of her desire to eat.

When someone wears tight clothing, they sometimes feel larger than they actually are. A wise person will not assume that they are large because they understand the feeling is a result of the tight pants. Remembering the size of their pants helps them let go of the feeling that they are large.

When a person is overweight, they may be sad and feel like a failure. A Drama Queen will feel bad and let that feeling take her over. A wise overweight person will understand that although she is overweight now, as long as she continues to eat well and exercise, being overweight is temporary. She will let go of the sadness and rejoice in the fact that she is healthy. She knows that what her body can do is more important than what it looks like.

The following questions will help you identify three unhealthy experiences and help you develop skills to better "let go" of them.

A. Describe a thought that makes you feel the worst about yourself.

_____
_____
_____

What is a healthy activity or thought pattern that can help you become wiser and "let go" of this negativity?

_____
_____
_____

B. Describe a feeling that makes you feel the worst about yourself.

_____
_____
_____

What is a healthy activity or thought pattern that can help you become wiser and "let go" of this negativity?

_____
_____
_____

C. Describe something you do that makes you feel the worst about yourself.

_____

_____

_____

What is a healthy activity or thought pattern that can help you become wiser and "let go" of this negativity?

_____

_____

_____

5. Wise People Focus on Inner Beauty

Since Drama Queens lack mature social skills, they feel insecure a lot. But because they are immature, they don't know how to express it or cope with it. When they feel insecure, they focus on their appearance or how popular they are.

A Drama Queen reminds herself that she is beautiful by flirting with the person she knows you have a crush on. Drama Queens may ask your best friend to go shopping, and forget to ask you. A Drama Queen will invite you to her party, knowing that it's on the same night as yours. Drama Queens can't discuss fashion without mentioning pant sizes and using words like "skinny" or "fat." Drama Queens say that they feel "fat," without realizing that every person that heard them will feel fat too.

I'd like to be like . . .

Hilary Hahn

A Grammy Award–winning violinist, Hahn was named "America's Best" young classical musician by *Time Magazine* when she was 22. She regularly plays with the world's great orchestras.

An important thing for you to remember is that inner beauty shapes outward beauty. Your personality is much more valuable and special than your outward looks. Making others feel special and being kind holds more beauty than blonde hair and blue eyes. A person is only as beautiful as their personality.

When your eyes gaze upon an outwardly beautiful person, it can be easy to forget that inner beauty is more valuable. The following scenarios can help you be mindful and remember that beauty is more than skin deep. What do you think about the difference between the wise and unwise reactions in these scenarios?

Scenario One

You are at home in your room, enjoying your favorite teen magazine. As you flip through the pages, you find yourself pausing to look at the teen models. Next thing you know, you start feeling unattractive and overweight.

UNWISE

Thoughts: "I am so much larger than her." "I wish I was her."

Feelings: "I feel fat." "I feel ugly." "I hate food."

Behavior: "I think I'll go on a diet."

WISE

Thoughts: "Are these images even realistic?"

Feelings: "It's so unfair that we are made to believe that these images are real!"

"It's so liberating to realize that these images aren't real!"

Behavior: "I don't think I'll buy this magazine anymore."

Scenario Two

You're watching your favorite TV show and realize that all the girls in the show are much smaller than you are and they are well-liked by just about every boy in the show.

UNWISE

    Thoughts: "Boys only like small girls."

    Feelings: "I feel lonely."

    Behavior: "I want to make myself smaller."

WISE

    Thoughts: "Healthy boys like healthy looking girls."

    Feelings: "I feel attractive because I am cute and kind."

    Behavior: "I think I'll organize a pizza party for my friends."

Scenario Three

You're walking down the hallway at school and you notice a classmate, who is very petite, gazing into her boyfriend's eyes. As you walk by you not only wish you were her, you feel unbearably unattractive.

UNWISE

    Thoughts: "Boys will never like someone like me." "I wish I looked like her."

    Feelings: "I feel fat, sad, and lonely."

    Behavior: "I think I'll skip lunch."

WISE

    Thoughts: "I wonder what her personality is like?"

                      "I wonder if she's as good a friend as I am?"

    Feelings: "I wouldn't trade anything I have for so-called great looks."

    Behavior: "I think I'll help my friend Sara study for her test."

In the next two pages, describe three scenarios that make you feel unwise. For each, outline the mindful and unmindful thoughts, feelings, and behaviors.

My Scenario One

_____
_____
_____

UNWISE

Thoughts: _____
_____

Feelings: _____
_____

Behaviors: _____
_____

WISE

Thoughts: _____
_____

Feelings: _____
_____

Behaviors: _____
_____

My Scenario Two

_____
_____
_____

UNWISE

Thoughts: _____
_____

Feelings: _____
_____

Behaviors: _____
_____

WISE

Thoughts: _____

_____

Feelings: _____

_____

Behaviors: _____

_____

My Scenario Three

_____

_____

_____

UNWISE

Thoughts: _____

_____

Feelings: _____

_____

Behaviors: _____

_____

WISE

Thoughts: _____

_____

Feelings: _____

_____

Behaviors: _____

_____

Things I Want to Remember

_____

_____

_____

_____

_____

_____

_____

_____

_____

_____

_____

_____

I'd like to be like . . .

Maya Lin

American artist and author who won the design competition for the Washington, D.C., Vietnam Veterans Memorial when she was a 21-year-old undergrad at Yale.

CHAPTER 6

Beautiful Girls

When it comes to standards of physical beauty, messages in the media are often confusing and misleading. We're shown a tall, white, blonde with perfect skin, and we're expected to think— *that's* what "beautiful" is. We enter a clothing store and see a beautiful outfit on such a person and think, "Wow that's beautiful. I want to be that beautiful. Maybe I can buy that beauty." So you buy the outfit.

Then later, looking in the mirror with your new outfit on, you may not feel as beautiful as the model—even though you *do* look beautiful. If you don't feel beautiful, you're probably comparing yourself to an illusion. Stop doing that! Just look at what's actually there in the mirror; stop comparing . . . and just take pleasure in the fact that "YOU ARE BEAUTIFUL!!"

And that's just at the physical level.

Inner beauty is deeper and more powerful physical beauty. At the physical level, it shines through whatever you wear. It's also better and more lasting than anything physical.

Have you ever met a person who just makes you feel good? The kind of person you enjoy being around? Someone who makes you laugh, or makes everyone feel important? When you look at that person, do you ever think, "She is so beautiful." If you don't, maybe you will after you read this chapter.

This chapter can start you on a journey of seeing and valuing inner beauty. I say journey because that is exactly what it is. Every day for the rest of your life, you will learn more about inner beauty. You will add to your list of qualities that make a person beautiful. You also will, maybe sadly, add to your list of things that *don't* make a person internally beautiful. Beauty isn't a number, a brand name, or a hairstyle. Rather than think, "She's the most beautiful person in my school," we'd like you to think, "There are many beautiful people in my school and they're all beautiful for different reasons." Inner beauty is unique to each person and much more than skin deep. Try thinking about that the next time you look in the mirror.

Our society places unrealistic expectations on women about beauty. Since these so-called ideals are unattainable, girls trying to attain them are literally getting sick from trying. We need a new way of thinking about beauty that gives us something to strive for that's actually attainable. You are beautiful today, and you can be even more beautiful tomorrow.

Sophie the Actress

Sophie is a member of the drama club and enjoys comedy TV. She has starred in a number of school plays and enjoys the spotlight. But the best part about Sophie is that she takes people into the spotlight with her! Whenever you need to feel special, Sophie is the perfect ticket to where you want to be. Like my birthday last year. I didn't think it was a big deal, but Sophie took every opportunity to make it feel like *my* special day. She was so excited for me, she told the entire school. People I didn't even know were wishing me a Happy Birthday! Sophie made me feel so good about myself. What a beautiful person she is!

Do you know anyone like Sophie? If so, who is it? _____

What does she do that makes her beautiful?

_____

_____

_____

What can you do for someone else that would be "Sophie-like"?

Who is it and what could you do?

_____

_____

_____

Fill in the blank lines below when *you've* done something.

I am beautiful because I _____

Describe what you did to make someone feel good. Be sure to name the person.

_____

_____

_____

Latisha the Lifesaver

I'm Cindy, and I have a disability that makes me need special help at school. I hate large groups of people and I'm terrible at making conversation. I don't have nice clothes. To say the least, I'm shy. I get picked on . . . A LOT. My classmates call me names like "stupid" and "fashion plate."

One day I was in the lunchroom and couldn't find a seat. I got there late because I needed extra help in my last class. I was walking around the lunchroom alone, scanning the tables to find a seat. I was so hungry. But every time I found an open spot, other people at the table would call me names and refuse to let me sit at their table.

It seemed like forever until Latisha touched my arm and said, "Come with me, Cindy." She led me to her table, where there were nine other girls way prettier and smarter than I'll ever be. Latisha introduced me to all of her friends and said I can always sit at her table if I need to. It was the best lunch I've ever eaten. Latisha made me feel so good about myself. What a beautiful person she is.

Do you know anyone like Latisha? If so, who is it? _____

What does she do that makes her beautiful?

_____

_____

_____

What can you do for someone else that would be "Latisha-like"?
Who is it and what could you do?

_____

_____

_____

Fill in the blank lines below when *you've* done something.

I am beautiful because I _____

Describe what you did to make someone feel good. Be sure to name the person.

_____

_____

_____

Unselfish Yumi

One day I forgot to pack my lunch and wouldn't you know it, I had no money in my lunch account. "GREAT! And I'm starving!" I screeched. Then I sat at the lunch table and stared at other kids eating hamburgers, turkey sandwiches, and potato chips. There I sat, until Yumi tapped me on the shoulder and said, "Why aren't you eating? Do you feel OK? Do you need to go see the nurse?"

"No, I'm just fine," I said, "but I forgot my lunch and I have no money in my account." The next thing I knew, Yumi was walking toward me with a lunch tray full of goodies. "For me?" I asked.

"Of course, silly, and by the way," she said with a wink, "you owe me." Yumi not only helped me not be hungry, she also made me feel important. What a beautiful person she is.

Do you know anyone like Yumi? If so, who is it? _____

What does she do that makes her beautiful?

_____

_____

_____

What can you do for someone else that would be "Yumi-like"?
Who is it and what could you do?

_____

_____

_____

Fill in the blank lines below when _you've_ done something.

I am beautiful because I _____

Describe what you did to make someone feel good. Be sure to name the person.

_____

_____

_____

Tara the Listener

My mom is a very difficult person to get along with. She expects me to get A's all the time and wants me to play sports during all three seasons. My opinion doesn't matter. I can tell her "I'm tired" or "I don't want to" and she just makes me feel weak and stupid. When she looks at me, I always feel like I'm a disappointment to her.

Tara is my best friend. She listens to me when I feel bad. She understands me more than my own mother does. She doesn't tell me how to feel. She doesn't tell me what to do. She just listens, and sometimes she even listens when I know she's heard it all before. And when I need it most, she makes me laugh. She's my best friend. Tara makes me feel important. What a beautiful person she is.

Do you know anyone like Tara? If so, who is it? _____

What does she do that makes her beautiful?

_____

_____

_____

What can you do for someone else that would be "Tara-like"?

Who is it and what could you do?

_____

_____

_____

Fill in the blank lines below when you've done something.

I am beautiful because I _____

Describe what you did to make someone feel good. Be sure to name the person.

_____

_____

_____

Felicia the Good Sister

Felicia is my older sister and I don't know what I'd do without her. Our parents are going through a real nasty divorce. They can't even talk about the weather, let alone us kids. Whenever they talk, it turns into an argument. Sometimes the arguments get real bad and they scare me. But no matter where she is in the house, Felicia always finds me and plays with me while they're fighting. Even though I can still hear them yelling, Felicia makes it all better because I know she cares about me. Felicia makes me feel loved. What a beautiful person she is.

Do you know anyone like Felicia? If so, who is it? _____

What does she do that makes her beautiful?

_____

_____

_____

What can you do for someone else that would be "Felicia-like"?

Who is it and what could you do?

_____

_____

_____

Fill in the blank lines below when *you've* done something.

I am beautiful because I _____

Describe what you did to make someone feel good. Be sure to name the person.

_____

_____

Selfless Shania

Shania is amazing. She is the most together person I know. A few weeks ago she had a birthday sleepover and could only invite five friends. Linda wasn't invited and, during lunch last week, she had a fit about that. In front of the whole lunchroom, Linda called Shania names and even threatened to punch her out.

But all the while, Shania was polite and never once raised her voice. She even told Linda that she was sorry for not inviting her! Shania hadn't even done anything wrong, but her apology did help Linda calm down.

Shania doesn't blow things out of proportion and she is selfless. She would much rather calm someone down than get into insisting that the other person has no reason to be upset with her. What a beautiful person she is.

Do you know anyone like Shania? If so, who is it? _____

What does she do that makes her beautiful?

_____

_____

_____

What can you do for someone else that would be "Shania-like"?

Who is it and what could you do?

_____

_____

_____

Fill in the blank lines below when *you've* done something.

I am beautiful because I _____

Describe what you did to make someone feel good. Be sure to name the person.

_____

_____

_____

Appreciative Alicia

What I like best about Alicia is that she is thankful. Better yet, she tells people when she is thankful for them. I remember her birthday last year. She had a rather large party and everybody bought her a gift. Not only did she write personal thank-you notes, but in the notes she told people about their special qualities and how much she appreciates their friendship! Who does that? I'm lucky if I even remember to say thank-you when I get a gift, let alone write a personal note. I love Alicia's thank-you notes because they make me feel so good about myself. Alicia always expresses appreciation for others. She even thanks boys for holding the door open for her. I know that if I do something nice for her, it will never go unnoticed. What a beautiful person she is.

Do you know anyone like Alicia? If so, who is it? _____

What does she do that makes her beautiful?

_____

_____

_____

What can you do for someone else that would be "Alicia-like"?

Who is it and what could you do?

_____

_____

_____

Fill in the blank lines below when _you've_ done something.

I am beautiful because I _____

Describe what you did to make someone feel good. Be sure to name the person.

_____

_____

_____

Loyal Lauren

I'm a nurse at a local nursing home, and I want to tell you about Lauren and her grandmother, Grace. Grace is eighty-five years old and lives at the home. She misses her house and talks about it a lot. She misses the opportunity to cook and bake like she used to, especially for her grandchildren.

Lauren is in her teens and is Grace's granddaughter. She visits Grace every day after school. They have beautiful chats about long summer days from the past and how they used to bake and cook together. Lauren sometimes uses her grandmother's recipes and bakes Grace a batch of something sweet and tasty. On those days, it seems that the aroma of the brownies or cookies or cake or whatever it is swoops Grace back in time to a happier place in her life. She smiles for days after those visits.

But best of all, during every visit I overhear Lauren telling her grandmother how thankful she is to have her in her life. Lauren helps Grace remember all of the little things that Grace used to do for her. Lauren celebrates her family and shows her appreciation for them by re-living their warm memories of her childhood with them. What a beautiful person Lauren is.

Do you know anyone like Lauren? If so, who is it? _____

What does she do that makes her beautiful?

_____

_____

_____

What can you do for someone else that would be "Lauren-like"?

Who is it and what could you do?

_____

_____

_____

Fill in the blank lines below when _you've_ done something.

I am beautiful because I _____

Describe what you did to make someone feel good. Be sure to name the person.

_____

_____

_____

Musical Mia

It was almost the end of the school year and we went to a school orchestra concert that my older sister was in. The music was so beautiful that I could hardly walk afterward. I felt like my feet didn't touch the ground. "I want to play in an orchestra someday," I told my Mom when we got to the car.

"Maybe in a few years, dear; but you have to practice every day to be able to play in the orchestra." I knew already that I wanted to play the French horn, but it took a week for my parents to rent one we could afford. I started practicing that very day, trying to get a sound.

Every day for the next four years I played in our school band and practiced in my room, preparing to audition for the orchestra. You had to be in high school to be in the orchestra, and I didn't want to miss a minute of it when my chance came. When the big day was finally here, I tried out and made it! I was a member of the school orchestra!

The next June, my dream came true, and all my practicing paid off. I performed in the concert at the end of that school year—with a small solo even! Right after the concert, my mother said, "Mia, I'm so proud of how you played tonight! The music was beautiful! But what I'm most proud of is how you made yourself practice every day for the past four years. That's something to be proud of all in itself—to be able to stick with something for your own future like that. You are such a beautiful girl."

Do you know anyone like Mia? If so, who is it? _____

What does she do that makes her beautiful?

_____

_____

_____

What can you do for someone else that would be "Mia-like"?
Who is it and what could you do?

_____

_____

_____

Fill in the blank lines below when *you've* done something.

I am beautiful because I _____

Describe what you did to make someone feel good. Be sure to name the person.

_____
_____
_____

My "Big Sister" Bianca

I'm Molly and I'm five. I live with my grandma because my mom can't take care of me. I love my grandma and all but she's old and can't move around much. I appreciate her taking care of me, but sometimes I'm bored. That's where Bianca comes in.

I'm a member of "Big Brothers / Big Sisters" and Bianca is my big sister. She isn't really my sister but she does things with me like a big sister would. She takes me to the mall to go shopping, she teaches me about friends, takes me to the movies, stuff like that. Last week she taught me how to play lacrosse! Very cool.

I so look forward to seeing Bianca every week. I love her. She is such a beautiful person.

Do you know anyone like Bianca? If so, who is it? _____

What does she do that makes her beautiful?

_____
_____
_____

What can you do for someone else that would be "Bianca-like"?
Who is it and what could you do?

_____
_____
_____

Fill in the blank lines below when *you've* done something.

I am beautiful because I _____

Describe what you did to make someone feel good. Be sure to name the person.

_____

_____

_____

Totally Awesome Katie

A few years ago, Katie's parents split up. Katie took it real hard. She didn't show it as much as her older sister did, but she felt every bit as awful.

Katie could tell that her mom also felt very, very bad. Instead of being mad at her, like her big sister was most of the time, Katie tried to help her mom when she could. But it never got easy: one big challenge after another seemed to come up for them, while her dad's new family seemed to have things a lot easier. Katie's older sister was cutting herself for a while, and then quit school before graduating—to live with some of her friends in another state.

Today was Katie's mom's birthday. You will not _believe_ what she did. First she read a poem she wrote for her mom, saying how much she loves her and how awesome she is, and how much she _knows_ now from all this stuff they've been through together. Then she sang an amazing birthday song, thanking her mom for sticking with her through thick and thin, like she knows they will all their lives for each other.

I couldn't believe _anyone_ could actually do that—out loud, in front of everyone! She is an incredibly beautiful person. The adults all had tears in their eyes!

Do you know anyone like Katie? If so, who is it?   _____

What does she do that makes her beautiful?

_____

_____

What can you do for someone else that would be "Katie-like"?
Who is it and what could you do?

_____

_____

_____

Fill in the blank lines below when *you've* **done something.**

I am beautiful because I _____

Describe what you did to make someone feel good. Be sure to name the person.

_____

_____

_____

Someone whose inner beauty inspires you

What story do you have to tell about inner beauty in people you know? Use this same format if it helps you see what you like so much.

My Beautiful, Inspiring Friend _____

What does _____ **do that makes her beautiful?**

_____

_____

_____

What can you do for someone that would be " _____ **-like"?**

_____

_____

_____

Fill in the blank lines below when *you've* **done something.**

I am beautiful because I _____

Describe what you did to make someone feel good. Be sure to name the person.

_____

_____

_____

Write as many stories like this as you want to that help you appreciate someone's inner beauty and develop that quality in yourself. Feel free to modify the structure however it helps you radiate!

Things I Want to Remember

CHAPTER 7

Do I Really Feel Bad About Myself?

Or did I just finish reading a teen magazine?

Teen and fashion magazines are loaded with brightly colored visuals of girls with absolutely perfect dimensions and flawless skin wearing or using a product that (they claim) can make *you* feel better.

First there are the products, which promise that you will feel better about yourself: leg moisturizers, pimple cream, sculpting gel, hair straighteners, razors, rollers, liquid foundation, powder foundation, eye shadow, eyeliner, lipstick, lip gloss, concealers, curling irons, flat irons, teeth whiteners, face brighteners, nail polish, nail art, the list goes on and on.

Then there are the fashion ads trying to get you to buy that special piece of clothing that will make you feel more attractive: bikinis, bras, underwear, sneakers, clogs, high heels, flats, denim jeans, straight leg jeans, stretch jeans, apple bottom jeans, prom dresses, t-shirt dresses, t-skirts, t-shirts . . . It's hard to stay caught up with styles that are deliberately changed so quickly.

And then there are the articles that promise to make you a better person. "The #1 Secret to a Great Body," "How to Get Perfect Skin, even when you break out," "485 Fashion Ideas," "If You Love Your Body Flaunt It," "How to Become Famous on MySpace," "How to Get a Tattoo the Safe Way," "What is Sexy?" "How to Find Out if You Know Who Your BFF Is". . .

For girls who worry about how to be accepted, many of these magazines are breeding grounds for poor mental and physical health habits. They can even make girls with good self-esteem feel crappy about themselves. This chapter will help you read these magazines and still feel good about who you are and the limits of your natural body.

Becoming "media literate" (and what is that, exactly???)

Media literacy begins with seeing that lots of people are trying to make you think you'll feel better about yourself if you buy their products. Being "media literate" means seeing what's going on, not being mindlessly manipulated, and making your own decisions about how you're affected by what they're trying to sell.

This is not easy to do—partly because so many people around you have already been "sold." Your chance of being able to take charge here is much better if you get some help. Your friends may be able to help. Your parent(s) and/or other adult allies may be able to help. The more help you can get, the better chance you have of becoming free from unhealthy media influences.

Now THAT'S a *great* thing to feel good about yourself for!

So we've written this chapter in a way that lets you invite a parent or any other helpful adult to team up with you. Or not. It could also be someone who isn't being helpful now, but may become helpful if they see what you're learning here. Or not.

Unfortunately, we live in a world where people make money by making you feel you need to be "prettier," "sexier," and more fashionable. Adults are also made to think they have to be younger looking, or richer, or have better cars and houses than other people. In this kind of world, becoming media literate is as important as anything you can do.

Messing with your mind

What follows are five advertising (brainwashing) techniques that have the same result: making you feel unattractive. We pair our discussion of each technique with an activity that helps you become aware of how these advertisements do it. Many of us flip through these magazines in a trance-like state. Not good. The activities help you change your experience of reading these magazines from a brainwashing experience into a conscious and mindful activity. You'll see how they try to make you think or feel something, even though you may not even realize it.

Brainwashing Technique No. 1

NOW YOU SEE IT, NOW YOU DON'T—THE MAGIC OF AIRBRUSHING

As we showed on page 17, YouTube has a 74-second video of how an everyday, ordinary-looking female is transformed into a person with model-like good looks. It is a fabulous demonstration of the power of media manipulation. Before your very eyes you see this her neck get longer and thinner, her eyes become larger and brighter, and her smile become wider and more perfect. In 74 seconds she goes from looking like you and us (many years ago), to looking like a runway model.

SEE:
www.youtube.com/
watch?v=hiby
AJOSW8U&NR=1

This next activity is for people who enjoy playing with computer images. You can do it with a variety of programs that let you manipulate images. If that doesn't sound interesting to you, skip this activity and go to the next. I did what you see below with Print Shop, by Adobe.

With whatever software you have or can get (or use on a friend's computer), follow its instructions to edit a photo of your choice. There's a really good FREE image-manipulating program called GIMP, and you can get it at www.gimp.org. CG-Pixel also offers a cool demo at http://cg-pixel.com/photo-retouching.html of how it's done in Photoshop. (Scroll down to the two images of the same teenage girl, click on the image, and try all three "pages.")

Here is an example of airbrushing I did on my home PC. On the left is the "before" picture which is just a picture I downloaded from a website. Notice the acne scars and the dark circles under her eyes.

What a little airbrushing can do—the acne and dark circles have magically disappeared!

ACTIVITY

Now let's have some fun. Load any picture of your choice and do some magic. Make your mom look younger. Make your dad look stronger. Make your brother look like a girl. Make your friend look like a beauty queen. Then next time you read a teen or fashion magazine, remember that *you* can make anyone look better, younger, thinner, or stronger . . .

Brainwashing Technique No. 2

"PERFECT" PEOPLE FLAUNTING THEIR PERFECTION

How is anyone supposed to feel attractive after looking at page after page of "perfection"? Teenage girls in bikinis with long legs, the "perfect-sized" hips, and "perfectly" round breasts. One article has a girl showing off a short skirt with a caption that says she loves that her legs are long, because it makes wearing skirts so much fun! The implication is that only girls with long legs can really have fun wearing a skirt. I estimate that only five to ten percent of readers will emerge from reading a teen magazine and still have a positive body image. It's as if you only compared your grades to whoever was best in each of your classes. You may never feel proud enough of your own efforts, no matter how good your grades.

Why not show normal looking females flaunting solutions to their imperfections? A healthy message could be "We're all imperfect, here's how you work with it." It could give tips on how to know your body type and how to choose clothing that accentuates the positive and de-emphasizes the not so positive.

> **Actress
> Tilda Swinton
> says no to makeup!**
> www.nytimes.com/
> indexes/2008/04/13/style/t/
> index.html#pageName=
> 13tildaw

ACTIVITY

First, take a look at the collages below. They are made from images cut from ads in a fashion magazine, plus the creator's own comments.

Now make one of these yourself from ads in a fashion or teen magazine (make sure it's yours or okay with the owner). Cut out pictures of perfect people flaunting their perfection, and make a collage on a piece of paper or other backing.

How do you feel when you look at each of these pictures?

List at least four feelings below.

1. _____

2. _____

3. _____

4. _____

Now write a healthy commentary over your collage. Use a thick marker, a hand-written note, a typed statement, or whatever you like. The commentary should be a truthful statement that helps remind you that these pictures are attempting to make you feel bad about yourself. Examples of a healthy commentary include "Why bother comparing myself to these girls, I'll never feel up to par," or "These images are airbrushed—these girls don't really look like that."

Brainwashing Technique No. 3

THE PROMISE OF LOOKING OLDER AND SEXIER

First, do you really *want* to look older and sexier? At this moment I'm looking at an advertisement for jeans. It's a full page ad showing a very thin woman with short cut-off jeans on and a shirt that rises to her midriff. And heels—red. This is a teen magazine and this model looks about 25 and *sexy*. The result—you may think to yourself something like: "If I don't look older or sexy, I'm not as beautiful as I could be. Maybe these jeans can help me feel better."

ACTIVITY

From a fashion or teen magazine, cut out pictures or articles that suggest you should feel sexy or look older and make a collage.

How do you feel when you look at each of the pictures you selected?
List at least four feelings.

1. _____

2. _____

3. _____

4. _____

Now write some healthy remarks over your collage—with a thick marker, a handwritten note, typed statement, whatever. It should be a truthful statement and remind you specifically how these pictures make you feel bad about yourself. Examples of a healthy commentary include: "If I actually was wearing that outfit to school what would my friends think?" "What would the boys say?" "I really don't want to look *that* sexy, do I?"

Brainwashing Technique No. 4

WAIF-LIKE AND GAUNT LOOKING WOMEN DESCRIBED AS BEAUTIFUL

Once I was looking at a teen magazine with my husband sitting next to me. "Oh my God!" he said.

There was picture of a sickly looking young woman in an ad for a line of clothing. I turned the page and there she was again . . . and again . . . eight pages of this young millionaire who looked like she needed to be in a hospital.

ACTIVITY

From a fashion or teen magazine, cut out pictures of waif-like women or girls and make a collage.

How do you feel when you look at each of these pictures? List at least four feelings.

1. _____
2. _____
3. _____
4. _____

Now write healthy commentary over your collage. Again, make truthful statement(s) that remind you that these pictures are trying to make you feel bad about yourself. Examples of a healthy commentary include "I never want to be that thin because I don't think it's attractive" "This model had to do terribly unhealthy things to herself to look this way" "I want to be healthy not gaunt."

Brainwashing Technique No. 5

USING "SKINNY" OR "THIN" AS DESIRABLE

One ad for a well-known line of hair products describes the girls in the picture as "hooked on super skinny serum." Another features a very thin young woman with her side midriff exposed. Then the articles: "The #1 Secret to a Great Body," "Get your Body Ready for Beach Season." Too much emphasis on thinness, not enough emphasis on health.

> **France says no to ultra-skinny models!**
> www.msnbc.msn.com/
> id/24126072/

ACTIVITY

From a fashion or teen magazine, cut out pictures or articles which use the words "skinny," "thin," or "weight loss" and make a collage.

How do you feel when you look at each of these pictures?
List at least four feelings.

1. _____
2. _____
3. _____
4. _____

Now write a healthy commentary over your collage that helps remind you that these pictures are attempting to make you feel bad about yourself. Examples of healthy commentary include "Being skinny doesn't necessarily mean I'm healthy" "Physical beauty can be airbrushed, inner beauty is real" "I want to be healthy not skinny."

I'd like to be like . . .

J.K. Rowling

Author of the famous and best-selling Harry Potter series. "I am an extraordinarily lucky person, doing what I love best in the world. I'm sure that I will always be a writer."

Ten things you can do together

Here are ten things you can do to help yourself and adults you care about.

1. **Talk about advertisements you see on TV and in magazines.** Regardless of whether the media directly influences you or if you talk with someone who is brainwashed by commercialized media, you may not realize you need help. Don't hesitate to initiate the discussion about media literacy with someone who may be able to help if you are confused or have some false impressions. "Is it true that the fashion industry makes millions of dollars by making us feel we need to be more attractive?" "Did you know that feeling unattractive makes us five times more likely to develop unhealthy eating habits?" Ask yourself and them questions like "How do I/you feel about how I/you look?" or "Are there any people or places that make me/you feel fat or unattractive?"

2. **Be careful not to toss around words like "fat" or "diet" in your home.** Slips of the tongue are easy to do when trying on your "skinny jeans" after the holidays. If someone says it out loud, it's more than likely that whoever hears them will feel fat too. Even during those times when you're not feeling so good about your shape, show restraint and keep it to yourself. Some households treat such terms as seriously as the use of swearing and profanities.

3. **Rather than talk about your appearance, focus conversations on health.** In a diet-obsessed world, it's *so* easy to lose perspective and forget that the goal is to live longer in good health. Part of the good news for heavy-set people who are not obese, but would like to lose a few pounds, is that statistics say you are likely to be perfectly healthy and live a long life. If you are free from illness and are not obese, keep your body dissatisfaction to yourself, and eat and exercise to live as long as possible—not so you can look better or fit into some once-favorite sweater you've outgrown!

4. **Discuss conversations you hear at school about appearance, beauty, or being slim.** School lunch tables are a breeding ground for what researchers have called "fat-talk." "Fat-talk" is a dialogue between kids that leads to unhealthy eating behavior or a negative body image: "Guess what, I'm wearing a size 4," or "Why are you eating that, it will just make you fat." Just overhearing these conversations can change your thought patterns and self-esteem. Ask your helpful (or would-be helpful) adult to check in with you about what kids are talking

about at school especially if you're confused by things you hear at school, on the bus, or in the locker room. If an overweight child is being picked on, ask the adult to help you find the right way to tell a school professional and or other adult at school.

5. **Review this workbook together from time-to-time.** Rather than to let it sit on a shelf and collect dust, use this book as a companion on your journey through the impressionable years in front of you. Ask your parent or adult friend to read the book with you and help you with some of the pen and pencil exercises. As you open up lines of communication together, you may find that certain sections help them help you with the exact topic that you or they are struggling with or have struggled with. Be flexible with this book and use it to fill a need, rather than be just another chore to complete.

6. **Remember that increasing self-esteem can feel like a fishing expedition.** The most common problem among young people today is how to have higher self-esteem. Low self-esteem can come from just about anywhere. Social interactions at home, in school, on the phone, or while IM'ing can all make you feel "less than." Figuring out what caused the change can sometimes feel like a fishing expedition. Ask the person helping you to ask you a question they think might lead somewhere. They may not come up with anything, but at least you'll know you tried. After enough casts, they may hit the right topic to help you catch a missing piece of your self-esteem.

7. **Seize the moment when you show a sign of body-image dissatisfaction.** It may be a passing comment or something you say under your breath while looking in the mirror. These little things should be immediately addressed. To wait, just increases the likelihood that you'll say, "Oh, it's nothing," or "I didn't mean it," or "I never said that." So seize the moment and inquire on the spot. Ask the person helping you to help you catch yourself at this. Give them permission to say: "Did I hear you right?" or "What did you mean when you said that?" or "What in the world makes you feel that way?" Then you can either talk about it or not; the important thing is to catch yourself at it so you can stop doing it to yourself.

8. **Ask your parent or adult friend to talk to other parents and coaches, no matter what the consequences.** They probably are amazed at the number of times one of your overnight guests opens up and shares something that makes their

mouth drop open. "My mom and I are having a contest to see who can lose five pounds first." "My mom says that pizza goes right to her hips and that I should never eat it. Do you have anything else for dinner?" "Coach Jackson says that I'd be a better gymnast if I could lose a few pounds." Even if it requires an uncomfortable phone conversation, you and your friend will both benefit from someone who's respected kindly asking that these harmful comments stop.

9. **Share your fears of becoming obese, if you have any.** With so much emphasis on obesity in the schools, some children are being scared into unhealthy anxiety or a distorted body image. Not everyone needs to hear about it. You may be hearing things that aren't intended for you, and taking the wrong message home. If you discuss your fears with the person helping you, you may be able to clear this up.

10. **When all else fails, listen with your whole heart when your parents tell you that they love you more than life itself.** Know that they just want *you* to see all the beauty in yourself that they do. This speaks for itself.

Things I Want to Remember

_____

_____

_____

_____

_____

_____

_____

_____

_____

_____

_____

_____

My Daily Food Journal

Date: _____

Time	Food and Amount	Mood

Describe your day today—especially in regards to how you were feeling throughout the day. Include both comfortable and uncomfortable feelings.

My Daily Activity Journal

Date: _____

Goal: This week I will try _____ (activity).

Goal: I will get physical activity on _____ days this week.

My Daily Activity Log

Time	Activity and Duration	Mood

My Hunger and Fullness Scale

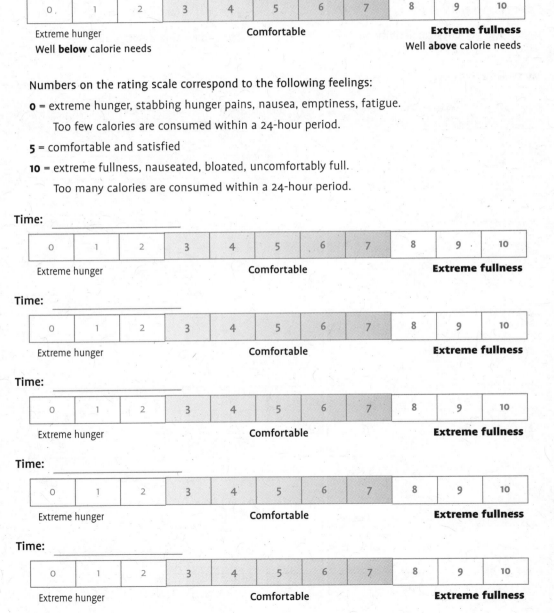

The Hunger and Fullness Scale

			The Ideal Range							
0	1	2	3	4	5	6	7	8	9	10

Extreme hunger   Comfortable   **Extreme fullness**

Well **below** calorie needs   Well **above** calorie needs

Numbers on the rating scale correspond to the following feelings:

0 = extreme hunger, stabbing hunger pains, nausea, emptiness, fatigue.

     Too few calories are consumed within a 24-hour period.

5 = comfortable and satisfied

10 = extreme fullness, nauseated, bloated, uncomfortably full.

     Too many calories are consumed within a 24-hour period.

Time: _____

0	1	2	3	4	5	6	7	8	9	10

Extreme hunger   Comfortable   **Extreme fullness**

Time: _____

0	1	2	3	4	5	6	7	8	9	10

Extreme hunger   Comfortable   **Extreme fullness**

Time: _____

0	1	2	3	4	5	6	7	8	9	10

Extreme hunger   Comfortable   **Extreme fullness**

Time: _____

0	1	2	3	4	5	6	7	8	9	10

Extreme hunger   Comfortable   **Extreme fullness**

Time: _____

0	1	2	3	4	5	6	7	8	9	10

Extreme hunger   Comfortable   **Extreme fullness**

My Problems and Coping Skills Journal

Here is the basic A-BE-C form to help you sort out who you will feel good about being in a stressful situation. See the examples that follow for special forms of applying it to situations involving sexuality, alcohol, and drugs.

1. Awareness & Insight: What Do I Need?
Describe a problem you have now.

_____
_____
_____

Who is the problem?

_____
_____

What is the problem?

_____
_____
_____
_____

Where is the problem?

_____
_____

Why is there a problem?

_____

_____

_____

When does the problem occur?

_____

_____

What do you need?

_____

_____

_____

_____

_____

2. Behavioral Control

Visualize the consequences of acting on your emotions right now. Describe:

_____

_____

_____

_____

_____

What are the real-life consequences of acting on the emotions you're having right now? Describe:

_____

_____

_____

How will the consequence feel?

_____

_____

_____

3. Emotional Expression

Describe how you feel regarding this situation when your feelings are most intense.

```
0                          5                          10
```

Unemotional   **Self-Awareness**

Overemotional

Ignoring feelings   Self-Control

Saying or doing things you regret

5 is the most productive place to be

How Do You Feel?

_____

_____

_____

_____

_____

_____

Not sure? Then:

Write in your journal

Talk with a friend or parent

Listen to music or read

Clarify how you feel and why

4. Communicating Needs

Develop a plan.

What do you want to say?

_____

_____

_____

_____

When do you want to say it?

_____

_____

_____

Focus on feelings because they can't be "wrong." How do you feel?

_____

_____

_____

_____

What does the person say/do that makes you feel bad?

_____

_____

_____

What changes can you both make to help the situation get better?

_____

_____

_____

_____

A-BE-C Sample Uses

Sexuality

What follows are examples of spelling out the A-BE-C's of situations involving sexuality. These are just two examples of many ways this model can help you feel good about yourself and how you act in situations that become confusing or stressful. When you do this for your own situations, be sure to adapt the questions in ways that fit your situation; always answer with your own true thoughts and feelings.

Example #1
Awareness and Insight

Describe the problem:

I'm stressed about how _____ [*say who*] wants to relate physically.

Who is the problem? _____ [*say who, same as above*]

What is the problem?

I feel pressure from _____ [*say who, same as above*] to do physical things with him/her that I don't feel good about.

Why is there a problem?

Possible answers:

I don't want to do what he/she wants, but I'm afraid that if I don't he/she won't like me.

I'm worried that if I do what he/she wants, other people will hear about it and not like me _____ [*say who will hear about it and not like you*]

I'm worried that if I do what he/she wants, I won't like him/her anymore.

I'm worried that if I do what he/she wants, I won't like me.

Maybe there's a problem because I'm not clear with him/her about what I really want?

Maybe there's a problem because I'm not clear about what I really want?

When/where does the problem happen?

Possible answers:

It happens at my house when he/she thinks no one will notice.

It happens at my house when no one else is home.

It happens at parties when he/she wants to impress people.

It happens at the movie theater.

It happens at _____.

What do I need?

Possible answers:

I need advice from _____ about this before it goes any further.

I need to figure out what I really want from _____ [*the "problem" person*].

I need to know if _____ [*the "problem" person*] is trying to use me or not.

I need to know if _____ [*the "problem" person*] really does care about me.

I need to know if _____ [*the "problem" person*] is someone I can trust.

I need to know if I'm someone I can trust in these situations.

I need _____.

Behavioral Control

Visualize the consequences of doing what he/she wants you to do:

Will doing it be harmful to you? Will you regret something later? What or how so?

Possible answers:

Not really. I think it will be good for me. I'll be happy that I did it and will want to do it again.

I won't feel good about having done something I'm not comfortable with.

I'll feel really vulnerable, like he/she could break my heart.

My reputation might get affected in a bad way.

Can I catch anything bad from doing that?

Will you hurt someone's feelings? Whose?

Possible answers:

If _____ [*my mom/dad? or ?*] finds out she/he will feel like she/he's not being a good parent or role model for me.

If _____ [*another girl?*] finds out, she'll be very upset.

If _____ finds out he/she will be ashamed of me.

Is there a chance you could get disciplined for doing this? How?

Possible answers:

I might get grounded.

I might not be able to be at home alone with a friend.

I might not be allowed to see _____ [*the "problem" person*] for a while.

I might not be allowed to do things with _____ [*the "problem" person*] or any of his/her crowd at all.

How will you feel if you get disciplined in that way?

Possible answers:

I'll feel like it was totally worth it for getting to do what I did.

I'll feel like there's no way it's worth it.

I'll be ashamed.

I'll feel misunderstood.

I'll be thankful that someone is showing me where the boundaries are.

Emotional Expression

Describe how you feel about this situation when your feelings are the most intense?
How Do You Feel?

0	5	10
Unemotional	**Self-Awareness**	**Overemotional**
Ignoring feelings	Self-Control	Saying or doing things you regret

5 is the most productive place to be

How do you feel? And how intensely do you feel it?

Possible answers:

I get confused. I like _____ [*the "problem" person*], but I don't like him/her trying to make me do things I don't want to. I feel this at around level 7.

Maybe I want to do it, but not with him/her. Or at least not now. This is around 8.

I feel like I shouldn't make a decision about this when I feel so emotional or aroused. This is a 5.

I feel very afraid that he/she will break my heart. This is a 10.

If you aren't sure what you feel: Write in your journal, talk with a friend or parent, listen to music, or read something related to your problem—all to clarify how you feel and why.

Communicating Needs

Develop a plan.
What do you want to say?

Possible answer:

I can say something like this to him/her:

"_____, I really like being with you and doing things together, but I'm confused about this part. You say you really like me, but then you don't seem to care that I'm not comfortable about this. You don't seem to listen when I tell you that. When you keep pressuring me anyway, I start to think that you really don't care about me, but just about what you want. Actions speak louder than words."

When do you want to say it?

Possible answers:

Duh, like how about last week?

The next time we're alone.

At school tomorrow.

What changes can you both make to help the situation get better?

Possible answers:

I can be clear with myself about what I want and make that clear to him/her.

He/she can back off and respect my feelings about what I'm comfortable with.

We can figure out what other things we enjoy doing together and build our relationship on those things.

Example #2

Awareness and Insight

Describe the problem.

I'm stressed about how _____ [*someone—we'll say "Courtney's father" for this example*] looks at me.

Who is the problem? _____ [*Courtney's father*]

What is the problem?

When I go to Courtney's house, I hate the way her father stares at me. The other day he asked me to sit next to him on the couch while Courtney was in the bathroom. I really didn't want to do that.

Why is there a problem?

Possible answers:

It makes me feel uncomfortable.

Something feels yucky to me.

My warning lights are flashing.

When/where does the problem happen?

Possible answers:

It happens whenever I'm at Courtney's house lately.

It happens when he gives us a ride somewhere.

It happens every time I'm alone with him.

What do I need?

Possible answers:

I need to feel safe when I'm at Courtney's house.

I want to know if I'm imagining things or if there's a reason to be uncomfortable.

I need to know if I should be worried about Courtney's father.

I need to know if I can trust Courtney's father.

I need advice from _____ about this.

Behavioral Control

Visualize the consequences of acting on the emotions you're having about this:

Will doing or not doing what your emotions are telling you to do about this be harmful to you? How so?

Possible answers:

I may get in trouble for accusing him of something I'm just imagining.

He may get angry at me for embarrassing him if I tell somebody.

He may hurt me if I tell.

He may hurt me if I don't tell someone.

I may get involved in something with him that I become really ashamed of.

Will you regret something later?

I should never do anything that makes me feel uncomfortable.

If I'm feeling uncomfortable, something is wrong. It doesn't have to make sense and there doesn't have to be evidence for why I feel this way. I feel the way I feel and should accept that.

Sometimes feeling uncomfortable is a warning sign of danger, so it's important for me to pay attention to it. I really shouldn't ignore this feeling, or I may really regret it.

I may get involved in something with him that I become really ashamed of.

Will you hurt someone's feelings? Whose?

Possible answers:

I may hurt Courtney's father's feelings.

I may hurt Courtney's feelings.

Is there a chance you could get disciplined for doing this? How?

Possible answers:

I might get in trouble with my parents for accusing their friend.

I might have to apologize to Courtney's father.

I might not be allowed to go to Courtney's house.

No—this isn't about something I'm doing that I shouldn't be doing. I should not get disciplined for this. I won't get disciplined for this. My parents will be glad I told them.

Will it be my fault if I don't tell, and something bad happens?

How will you feel if you get disciplined in that way?

Possible answers:

I'll feel like it whoever would discipline me for this isn't paying attention to what's really happening.

I'll feel misunderstood.

I'll be very angry.

Emotional Expression

Describe how you feel about this situation when your feelings are the most intense?

How Do You Feel?

. . . .

0	5	10
Unemotional	**Self-Awareness**	**Overemotional**
Ignoring feelings	**Self-Control**	**Saying or doing things you regret**

5 is the most productive place to be

How do you feel? And how intensely do you feel it?

Possible answers:

I feel uncomfortable and afraid that I will lose my friend Courtney if anything bad happens. This is an 8.

I'm afraid of Courtney's father. This is a 10.

I'm very embarrassed to be in this situation. This is a 7.

I feel powerful. It's exciting. This is a 7.

If you aren't sure what you feel: Write in your journal, talk with a friend or parent, listen to music, or read something related to your problem—all to clarify how you feel and why.

Communicating Needs

Develop a plan.

What do you want to say, and to whom?

Possible answer:

I need help from an adult. I think I'll tell my mom (or my guidance counselor) that I feel uncomfortable at Courtney's house, and see where that leads to.

I'll tell Courtney I'd rather have us get together at my house, and hope she doesn't ask me why.

When do you want to say it?

Possible answers:

Duh, like how about last week?

The next time I can get a minute alone with my mom.

The next time Courtney invites me to her house.

What changes can you both make to help the situation get better?

Possible answers:

I don't know yet.

Someone has to help me figure this out.

Drugs, alcohol

Here's an example of getting to your A-BE-C's of a situation involving drugs or alcohol. This is just one example of how this approach can help you feel good about yourself and how you act in situations involving them. When you do this for your own situations, be sure to adapt the questions in ways that fit your situation; always answer with your own true thoughts and feelings.

Awareness and Insight

Describe the problem.

I'm feeling like I don't fit in at school. I feel alone a lot. I have a new group of friends I could join, but they want me to drink and do drugs with them. I don't really want to, but . . .

Who is the problem?

Possible answer:

_____ and _____ and their friends who I'd like to be friends with.

What is the problem?

Possible answer:

I want to fit in with _____ because they're cool; but I don't really want to drink or do drugs, and they want me to do that with them. I'm afraid that if I don't, I'll be a loner and a loser. I'm confused.

Why is there a problem?

Possible answer:

I don't know how to fit in and be friends with these kids without drinking or doing drugs, like they're asking me to. I don't really want to do either. But I don't want to be a loner or a loser.

When/where does the problem happen?

Possible answers:

It happens in people's houses after school.

It happens in a lot near the school, sometimes before school, and sometimes after.

It happens kind of everywhere I see them, because it affects how they think of me.

What do I need?

Possible answers:

I need to know if these things are really unhealthy or dangerous, or not.

I need a friend to talk about this with. It would be great if it could be someone who will like me whether I drink and do drugs or not.

I need someone to talk with who actually knows about alcohol and drugs, and has really good information about how they affect kids my age.

Behavioral Control

Visualize the consequences of doing or not doing these substances with these kids.

Will doing them be harmful to you? How so?

Possible answers:

They might do some damage to my body. I heard about _____.

They might make me do something weird or dangerous. I heard about _____.

Will not doing them be harmful to you? How so?

Possible answers:

Not to my body, no.

Maybe to how some people think of me—but I'm not really sure who will think what.

If they think I might tell on them they might do something weird to me.

Will you hurt someone's feelings? Whose?

Possible answers:

Maybe _____ and _____'s feelings, as they're the ones who invited me to do it with them.

If my mom/dad [or _____] finds out she/he will feel like she/he's not being a good parent.

If _____ finds out he/she will be ashamed of me.

Will you do something that you might regret later? What?

Possible answers:

If it really does mess up my brain or something else in my body, I'd regret that.

If I do it, maybe I'd do something stupid that people will tease me about for years?

If I don't do it, maybe they'll tease me about that for years.

What happens to us if the drugs are bad? How does anyone know if they are or not, anyway?

Is there a possibility that you could get disciplined for your behavior? How?

Possible answers:

If I get caught, I might get grounded.

I might not be allowed to hang out with these friends any more.

I might get in trouble with the police.

How will you feel if you get disciplined in that way?

Possible answers:

Stupid, because part of me already knows it's not a good idea for me.

Totally okay about it. I want this experience and it's worth the risk.

Emotional Expression

Describe how you feel about this situation when your feelings are the most intense?

How Do You Feel?

0	5	10
Unemotional	**Self-Awareness**	**Overemotional**
Ignoring feelings	Self-Control	Saying or doing things you regret

5 is the most productive place to be

How do you feel? And how intensely do you feel it?

> *Possible answers:*
>
> I feel completely confused. I've never thought of myself as a person who would do drugs—why am I even thinking about this? This is a 9.
>
> I feel like I lose either way. This is a 5.
>
> I feel sad. Why can't we find healthy ways to have fun? This is an 8.
>
> Part of me is excited by the risk, but another part is afraid of the danger. I'm not ready for this. This is a 5.

If you aren't sure what you feel: Write in your journal, talk with a friend or parent, listen to music, or read something related to your problem—all to clarify how you feel and why.

Communicating Needs

Develop a plan.

What do you want to say to _____ [*the people who asked you to drink and/or do drugs with them*]?

> *Possible answers*
>
> I'm just not ready for this. Can you give me some space to work it out on my own time?
>
> What do you like about this?
>
> Aren't you at all scared about this? Did you hear about _____?

When do you want to say it?

> *Possible answers:*
>
> The next time _____ brings it up.
>
> I'd like to call _____ and ask him/her to meet me _____ tomorrow so we can talk about how much I like them but how much I don't want to do this.

What changes can you both make to help the situation get better?

Possible answers:

I can try not to act like I know if it's as bad for them as I think it might be for me.

They can show that they care enough about me to let me work this out on my own in my own time.

Your blank sheet to fill in as you need to:

Awareness and Insight

Describe the problem:

_____
_____
_____
_____
_____
_____
_____
_____
_____
_____

Who is the problem?

_____
_____
_____

What is the problem?

_____
_____
_____
_____
_____

Why is there a problem?

_____

_____

_____

_____

When/where does the problem happen?

_____

_____

_____

_____

What do I need?

_____

_____

_____

_____

Behavioral Control

Visualize the consequences of doing xyz about the problem:

Will doing it be harmful to you? Will you regret something later? What or how so?

_____

_____

_____

_____

Will you hurt someone's feelings? Whose?

_____

_____

_____

Is there a chance you could get disciplined for doing this? How?

_____

_____

_____

_____

How will you feel if you get disciplined in that way?

_____

_____

_____

_____

Emotional Expression

Describe how you feel about this situation when your feelings are the most intense.

How Do You Feel?

0	5	10
Unemotional	**Self-Awareness**	**Overemotional**
Ignoring feelings	Self-Control	Saying or doing things you regret

5 is the most productive place to be

How do you feel? And how intensely do you feel it?

_____

_____

_____

If you aren't sure what you feel: Write in your journal, talk with a friend or parent, listen to music, or read something related to your problem—all to clarify how you feel and why.

Communicating Needs

Develop a plan.

What do you want to say?

_____

_____

_____

_____

_____

When do you want to say it?

_____

_____

_____

_____

_____

What changes can you both make to help the situation get better?

_____

_____

_____

_____

_____

Okay, Girls! Listen up . . .

You GROW Girl! is just the tip of the proverbial self-esteem iceberg. Being a kid is stressful: schoolwork, sports, drama queens, divorced parents, and sibling rivalry are just a few of the many burdens you cope with. If you're really serious about building your self-esteem, what follows will help you a lot. These are suggested books to read and web sites to visit on your journey toward being a confident and healthy young woman.

Sean Covey has a series of books and workbooks about the habits of highly effective people. His workbook, *The 7 Habits of Highly Effective Teens* (1999), offers many tools to help you reach your potential and develop skills such as time management and goal setting.

Chicken Soup for the Girl's Soul: Real Stories by Real Girls about Real Stuff, by Jack Canfield, Mark Victor Hansen, and Irene Dunlap (2005) is a friendly book that helps you understand the many feelings you experience day to day.

Beautiful Women: Celebrating Beauty in Stories and Stills, by Nancy Bruno (2008) is a short picture book that describes the life-struggles of women who are truly beautiful. It helps you deepen your understanding that beauty is more than skin deep.

No Body's Perfect: Stories by Teens about Body Image, Self-Acceptance, and the Search for Identity, by Kimberly Kirberger (2003) helps you understand why you feel fat. Each chapter is written by teens who are struggling with that feeling and talk about what it's like to live in a society in which body image is distorted and unhealthy.

The Body Project: An Intimate History of American Girls, by Joan Jacobs Brumberg shows how growing up in a female body has changed in the last hundred years, and why it's so much more difficult today than ever. Definitely for the adults in your life, and if you're a reader you'll just *love* it.

Over It: A Teens Guide to Getting Beyond Obsessions with Food and Weight, by Carol Emery Normandi, Lauralee Roark, and Kate Dillon (2001) is another helpful book for teens about body image.

If you have questions about what and how much a healthy teenager eats, *Fueling the Teen Machine*, by Ellen Shanley (2001) can be a great resource. *Healthy Eating for Life for Children*, by Neal Barnard & Amy Lanou, Physicians Committee for Responsible Medicine (2002), is another fine resource on this topic; this one is also very good for the adults in your life.

You may also get inspired by these terrific web sites

www.campaignforrealbeauty.com/home.asp

It rocks. Dove has brought together lots of very cool, fun-to-do stuff here for you and the adults in your life: self-esteem, body image, nutrition, and beauty issues.

www.ithaca.edu/looksharp/

Project Look Sharp—Media Literacy at Ithaca College. Offers multimedia literacy kits that are fun and very informative.

www.girlsontherun.org/default.html

Encourages preteen girls to develop self-respect and healthy lifestyles through running. Includes all aspects of development: physical, emotional, mental, social, and spiritual well-being.

www.girlscouts.org/program/program_opportunities/leadership/uniquelyme.asp

Created in 2002 to address the critical nationwide problem of low self-esteem among adolescent and pre-adolescent girls, uniquely ME!, the Girl Scout/Dove Self-Esteem Program, is designed to foster self-esteem in girls, ages 8–17.

www.opheliasplace.net

Ophelia's Place offers "a vision of providing a safe haven that is respectful and supportive of girls' voices, your feelings and your dreams." Also links to many very cool sites. Our favorites are:

Teen Voice: www.teenvoices.com

An online and print magazine by, for and about teen girls.

New Moon: www.newmoon.org

A magazine for girls and their dreams. Edited and created by and for girls ages 8–14. Commercial-free! Young writers & artists' submissions welcome.

Girls, Incorporated: www.girlsinc.org

A national organization that provides research-based after school curriculum and programs to help girls become smart, strong and bold.

GirlZone: www.girlzone.com

All kinds of great articles, advice, facts, and info about everything from sports to music to women's history, feminism, careers, money, books, etc.

Girl Scout Teen Empowerment: www.studio2b.org

Teen articles and info by the Girl Scouts, these are still interesting and useful for other girls as well.

Girlsite: www.girlstart.com

Math, science, games, stories about cool women, job information, etc.

Zoey's Room: www.zoeysroom.com

An interactive, educational website for girls 10–14. Math, science & technology. A $15 member fee ensures safe, private access for each girl, and one-on-one attention. (Suitable for adults to do with you—maybe they'd be willing to pay the fee?)

http://cg-pixel.com/photo-retouching.html

For that photo retouching exercise in chapter 7, this is the address to find the tutorial about how it's done in Photoshop. We don't know how much or how little it will help you with other software, but can it hurt to look?

www.insidebeauty.org/

Inside Beauty is an educational outreach program created by model Magali Amadei and body image expert Claire Mysko. Combining personal stories with real examples of photo retouching, their presentation gives girls and young women a healthy perspective on our culture's messages about beauty.

For the adults in your life . . .

Many of the resources mentioned above are also good to have the adults in your life know about. Some adults are actually at least a bit scared, and maybe even feel helpless, about not knowing enough about what their daughter or valued younger relative or friend needs. These resources can help them:

If a parent or adult in your life makes you feel fat or is constantly dieting, ask them to read *I'm Like So FAT!* by Dianne Neumark-Sztainer (2005). It will help that person understand the damage they can do to you without realizing it. It speaks to the dangers of dieting and shows the adult how to help you feel better about yourself and your body. We also recommend:

Weight Loss Confidential: How Teens Lose Weight and Keep It Off—and What They Wish Parents Knew, by Anne M. Fletcher and Holly Wyatt (2007)

The Body Image Workbook, by Thomas Cash (1997)

The Psychology of Eating: From Healthy to Disordered Behavior, by Jane Ogden (2002)

Preventing Eating Disorders among Pre-teens, by Beverly Neu Menassa (2004)

Understanding the Causes of a Negative Body Image, by Barbara Moe (1999)

The Body Project: an Intimate History of American Girls, by Joan Jacobs Brumberg (1998)

Fasting Girls: A History of Anorexia Nervosa, by Joan Jacobs Brumberg (2000)

Psychological Responses to Eating Disorders and Obesity: Recent and Innovative Work, by Julia Buckroyd and Sharon Rother (2008)

Fat Talk: What Girls and Their Parents Say about Dieting, by Mimi Nichter (2001)

The Parent's Guide to Childhood Eating Disorders, by Marcia Herrin and Nancy Matsumoto (2002)

Before She Gets Her Period: Talking to Your Daughter about Menstruation, by Jessica B. Gillooly (1998)

And . . .

Here are some of our favorite "Empowerment and Information" web resources for parents, guardians, educators and adult allies of girls . . .

www.zoeysroom.com

Zoey's Room: Worth mentioning twice, from above.

www.hardygirlshealthywomen.org

Hardy Girls Healthy Women: For parents, teens, and educators.

www.thebodypositive.org

Encourages people of all sizes to be physically active, eat healthily, and develop social support, self-respect, and a positive body image.

Acknowledgments

Kim and I have many people to thank as we enter the world of published authors:

Our publishers, Paul Cash and Amy Opperman Cash for seeing the potential in a modest spiral-bound manuscript, and for pushing us to and respecting our cognitive limits . . .

Joan Jacobs Brumberg for her intellect, wisdom, and generosity, and for her gracious and very helpful foreword to our book . . .

Laurie O'Shaughnesy, director of the Queensbury Parks and Recreation Department, whose enthusiasm and excitement about the You GROW Girl! idea have motivated us to persist as the YGG program gains momentum.

Four already very busy professionals who graciously made time to review our manuscript and offer great suggestions for making it better:

Myra Berkowitz, MNS, RD, CDN, Nutritionist at Cornell University Gannett Health Services, who has worked with college students on nutrition for physical and mental health since 1986.

Cynthia Scheibe, Associate Professor, developmental psychology, media literacy, Ithaca College; founder and executive director of Project Look Sharp, a media literacy initiative of DIIS that provides support, materials, and training for the integration of media literacy across the curriculum in K–12 and postsecondary education.

Janis Whitlock, Research Scientist in the Family Life Development Center at Cornell University.

Cris E. Haltom, Ph.D., Licensed Psychologist and Community Education Liaison, Eating Disorder Recovery Center of Western New York.

My colleagues at Osika & Scarano Psychological Services who have supported my writing endeavors for five years—Carmella Mayette, Theresa Pratt, and Anna Sadowski for their perfectionism and professionalism and ability to help me manage too many "balls in the air"... Sheryl Kirk who never once complained as work was literally thrown onto her desk. Thank you all from the bottom of my heart for keeping me on task and reminding me of details I forgot.

My sister Michele Harland, her husband Glenn, their daughters Maddie and Lindsay... you all have been inspiring models of family unity, strength, hope, and courage during Michele's sudden struggle with leukemia. You all provide the needed perspective when my busy life becomes nearly overwhelming.

Jenny Rovetto-Dean, L.C.S.W. and Todd Kuntz, Psy.D. for lessening my workload by graciously adjusting your own, so I could devote time and energy to my sister and her family. Thanks also for forgiving my lapses in memory, which certainly caused you confusion and frustration at times.

We'd like to thank Emily Draus for designing and formatting sample chapters we submitted to publishers for review. Your patience was remarkable!

God Bless my children, Tommy, Jerod, and Jonathan. You adjusted willingly to your weekends with dad, you listened to us, and you were encouraging when I seemed to be going nowhere. Through my entire experience as a new "writer," your sense of humor, angelic faces, and warm cuddles helped me remember what really matters. Remember: I will always view this book as a "family project."

The person I am most indebted to is my husband, Tom—life partner, business colleague, and father of our boys. This past year has been the most difficult in our nearly fifteen years of marriage, and I have never loved you more. You are the reason our business and our children have both emerged from this year unscathed.

—GINA SCARANO-OSIKA

I want to dedicate this book in loving memory of my dad, whose presence I feel in my heart every day like pennies from heaven.

To my Mother and sisters, thank you for many hours of entertaining our three energetic boys when deadlines needed to be met.

To my cousin Amy, a great source of laughter and joy in my life, your unstoppable wit and perspective are gems to me.

To Eric, my husband and best friend, your love, support, and humor keep me grounded and for that I am thankful. You are a wonderful husband and father to our boys Gregory, Michael, and Matthew.

—KIM DEVER-JOHNSON